M000265609

What Works!

What Works!

Successful Writing Strategies for National Board Certification

Bobbie Faulkner

ROWMAN & LITTLEFIELD
Lanham • Boulder • New York • Toronto • Plymouth, UK

Published by Rowman & Littlefield
4501 Forbes Boulevard, Suite 200, Lanham, Maryland 20706
www.rowman.com

10 Thornbury Road, Plymouth PL6 7PP, United Kingdom

Copyright © 2014 by Bobbie Faulkner

All rights reserved. No part of this book may be reproduced in any form or by any electronic or mechanical means, including information storage and retrieval systems, without written permission from the publisher, except by a reviewer who may quote passages in a review.

British Library Cataloguing in Publication Information Available

Library of Congress Cataloging-in-Publication Data

Faulkner, Bobbie, 1947– author.
What works! : successful writing strategies for National Board certification / Bobbie Faulkner.
p. cm.
Includes index.
ISBN 978-1-4758-0710-3 (cloth : alk. paper) — ISBN 978-1-4758-0711-0 (electronic)
1. Teachers—Certification—Standards—United States—Study guides. 2. Teaching—Standards—United States—Study guides. I. Title.
LB1771.F37 2014
379.1'57—dc23

2013046449

∞™ The paper used in this publication meets the minimum requirements of American National Standard for Information Sciences Permanence of Paper for Printed Library Materials, ANSI/NISO Z39.48-1992.

Printed in the United States of America

Contents

List of Figures

Preface

There have been two "generations" of the National Board Certification process to date. Generation 1 consisted of six entries and a full day of content-based Assessment Center exercises. Generation 2 is the current process (2013–2014) with four entries (some entries from Generation 1 were combined) and six content-based Assessment Center exercises.

Generation 3 is being developed at the time of this writing and will be unveiled in segments over the course of three years—2014 through 2017. Very basically, there will be four sections, called components, that will address student work, videos, and professional development. Content knowledge will be embedded into the modules. Components 1 and 2 will be released for the 2014–2015 cycle, Component 3 will be released for the 2015–2016 cycle, and Component 4 will be released last—for the 2016–2017 cycle. Details concerning the Assessment Center component are not yet determined. However, the foundational elements that are the core of the National Board Certification process, the Five Core Propositions, the Standards, the Architecture of Accomplished Teaching, and the Scoring Rubrics, will remain unchanged in the Generation 3 process.

If you are beginning your National Board journey during the 2013–2014 cycle *or* were a Take One! participant during or before 2013–2014 *or* are an Advanced Candidate, all information contained in this book is current and accurate for you. If you begin your National Board journey during the 2014–2015 cycle, much of this book's contents will still be applicable, but because the Generation 3 components are not available at this time, the author cannot address specifics beyond those already noted. Follow *your* cycle's instructions and directions.

Acknowledgments

I would like to offer special thanks to those who have contributed significantly to my National Board Certification journey. From Scottsdale I owe appreciation to Nancy Creighton Brown, former Career Ladder specialist, whose open mind and dedication to Scottsdale teachers allowed National Board Certification to take root and grow in Scottsdale. The core group of original facilitators of the Career Ladder cohorts, Debbie Voris, Mary Zongolowicz, Sharon Guttell, and Christine Hawes, are the epitome of passionate educators who have worked hard for this cause. In addition, I appreciate the vision that former superintendent Dr. John Baracy and the Governing Board demonstrated with their financial support of National Board Certified Teachers in Scottsdale. Three others who are instrumental to National Board Certification in the district are Dr. Andi Fourlis, assistant superintendent for excelling teaching and learning, Dr. Jeff Thomas, assistant superintendent of human resources, and current Career Ladder and professional development specialist Wendy Allen. A special thanks goes out to my NBCT cyber-friend from the Power of Accomplished Teaching website, Kelly Mueller, whose comments and suggestions were invaluable.

Finally, I want to acknowledge Dr. Kathy Wiebke, director of the Arizona K–12 Center, for her inspiration and dedication to the National Board Certification process in Arizona. Without her vision and passion, and that of her dedicated staff, Arizona would not now have over 800 NBCTs. They have been and continue to be beacons of light to Arizona educators.

Introduction

What Works! Successful Writing Strategies for Pursuing National Board Certification is the third in my *What Works!* series. It started with one of those off-the-cuff remarks that no one ever dreamed would actually amount to anything. "You ought to write a book," a fellow facilitator said one day after we finished a workshop for candidates. And that's what I did.

What Works! Successful Writing Strategies for Pursuing National Board Certification is meant to be a practical, user-friendly resource for candidates in all certificate areas. The information contained in its chapters comes largely from my own experience as a candidate and facilitator of candidates, study of the National Board Certification process, and the needs and frustrations that candidates themselves have expressed.

What Works! Successful Writing Strategies was written to be used as a supplement to the entire body of information and portfolio instructions provided to candidates from the National Board for Professional Teaching Standards (NBPTS). Information contained in the official NBPTS documents is always the final word and trumps any other source.

What Works! Successful Writing Strategies is *not* endorsed by the NBPTS or any other entity involved in the National Board Certification process. It is not meant to be a Cliff Notes–type publication that one can use to circumvent the NBPTS documents and instructions.

What Works! Successful Writing Strategies contains tips, opinions, information, documents, and examples that have been created solely for the purposes of demonstration and are neither approved nor endorsed by the NBPTS. Keep in mind that:

- The author is not a trained assessor and does not imply that any sample writing would score well and/or lead to certification according to the NBPTS portfolio rubrics.
- Writing samples are fabricated—*made up*—and are *not* from actual portfolio entries.
- Writing samples are for demonstration purposes only and may not reflect all guidelines and formatting suggested by the NBPTS. They *cannot* be copied or used in a portfolio.
- *What Works! Successful Writing Strategies* is as accurate and current as I could make it. However, portfolio directions and other requirements do change over time, and it is the responsibility of the candidate to be informed of the current NBPTS requirements.

What Works! Successful Writing Strategies is a labor of love for my fellow educators and National Board candidates, and it is my hope that using this book will make your journey to National Board Certification just a little easier.

Chapter One

What Is National Board Certification?

Six Word Memoir: Know your standards. Know them well! —Britney, NC

NBPTS BACKGROUND AND HISTORY

National Board Certification is a national *voluntary* system that certifies teachers who meet a set of high and rigorous standards for what accomplished teachers should know and be able to do. This certification system was developed by the National Board for Professional Teaching Standards (NBPTS) and put in place in 1987 following recommendations from the Carnegie reports "A Nation at Risk" and "A Nation Prepared."

The National Board has developed high, rigorous, research-based standards to measure the effectiveness of a teacher's practice. The process involves an extensive series of performance-based assessments that include teaching portfolios, student work samples, written commentaries, video recordings, and thorough analysis of the teacher's classroom practice and the impact on student learning. In addition, teachers complete a series of written exercises that probe their depth of knowledge of their subject matter.

The work is based on long-established research that identifies and recognizes sound educational practices that result in student learning. The NBPTS has commissioned more than 140 studies and papers on the value of the certification process as well as its standards and assessment. The process has also been validated by a number of independent studies.

THE FIVE CORE PROPOSITIONS

The Core Propositions are the heart of the National Board process. They outline the expectations and values for what *accomplished* teachers should know and be able to do, and are the umbrella under which the other elements of the National Board Certification process are organized. Accomplished teaching implies going *above and beyond* what is typically expected of the average teacher. The Propositions describe skills in the following areas:

- *Proposition 1: Commitment to Students*. Accomplished teachers know the developmental levels of their students, believe that all students can learn regardless of background, and use their knowledge to design effective instruction for all students and a variety of learning styles.

- *Proposition 2: Knowledge of Subject.* Building upon their knowledge of students, accomplished teachers advance their own understanding of their content area and develop a wide range of strategies to set high and worthwhile goals to teach that subject matter to their students.
- *Proposition 3: Manage and Monitor Student Learning.* Accomplished teachers understand how to manage, motivate, monitor, and assess student learning by planning appropriate learning sequences to achieve the desired outcomes and adjusting instruction as needed. Accomplished teachers also know how to structure the learning environment for optimum learning.
- *Proposition 4: Think Systematically about Their Teaching and Learn from Experience.* Accomplished teachers analyze student learning and reflect on their teaching practice. They then determine the next set of high and worthwhile goals, implement appropriate instruction, and continue the analysis and reflection cycle.
- *Proposition 5: Teachers Are Members of Learning Communities.* Accomplished teachers collaborate with other professionals, parents, and their larger community to support and enhance student learning.

THE STANDARDS

There are 25 certificates that cover many subject areas and student development levels. Each contains a set of Standards, which, along with the five Core Propositions, form the foundation of National Board Certification. The Standards identify specific knowledge, skills, and attitudes that support accomplished practice while emphasizing the holistic nature of teaching. They identify how a teacher's professional judgment is reflected in action, and they reflect the Five Core Propositions.

To achieve National Board Certification and be considered an accomplished teacher, a candidate must show *clear, convincing, and consistent* evidence that his or her teaching practice reflects the Standards. Understanding the Standards and how to demonstrate them in practice provides evidence of accomplished teaching.

What Works: Understanding Your Standards

- *Read* the Standards multiple times. Pay attention to the examples included in each.
- *Think* about how you already incorporate the Standards.
- *Highlight* things you already do regularly in one color, things you do sometimes in a second color, and things you rarely or never do in a third color. This will help you recognize your strengths and what might be bolstered in your practice.
- *Show* clear, consistent, convincing evidence that your teaching is based on the Standards.

Why It Works

The Standards were developed to identify accomplished teaching. Candidates are expected to show evidence of the Standards within their teaching.

THE PROCESS

National Board Certification is a rigorous process that may take up to three years to achieve. Candidates are asked to:

- *Demonstrate* within their teaching practice the rigorous Standards discussed above.
- *Show* leadership, collaboration, learning, reflective practice, and professionalism.
- *Prepare* a portfolio of four written entries that document their teaching practice.
- *Focus* on analysis of student work samples, classroom practice and professional development, collaboration, and leadership.
- *Make* videotapes of the teacher working with his or her class.
- *Complete* a series of subject specific written tests at an assessment center to document knowledge of their subject area.

National Board Certification is the highest, most comprehensive voluntary professional development experience available to teachers. Examining their teaching practice and professional accomplishments in depth provides teachers a professional growth experience unlike any other.

Chapter Two

Building Your Foundation

Six Word Memoir: The AAT: Backbone of Accomplished Lessons. —Russell, VT

WHO IS AN ACCOMPLISHED TEACHER?

In a nutshell, an accomplished teacher is one who goes *above and beyond* what is typically expected. Accomplished teachers practice exceptional, skilled teaching. They have a strong knowledge base of subject matter and pedagogy; demonstrate complex, nuanced professional work; and consistently meet rigorous standards of practice. Accomplished teachers are committed to their students, know their subjects and how to teach them, know how to manage and monitor student learning, reflect on their practice and learn from their experience, and are learners, collaborators, and leaders within their professional communities (the Five Core Propositions).

Accomplished teachers are teachers just like you, who try their best every day to meet their students' needs, keep current with pedagogy and subject knowledge, and work with others in their schools and districts to create an environment conducive to supporting the healthy growth and development of their students academically, socially, and emotionally.

WHAT IS ACCOMPLISHED TEACHING?

Accomplished teaching is the double helix of knowing your subject and how to teach it. The two strands are tightly entwined and seamlessly connected. Accomplished teaching combines both the art and craft of teaching along with a solid knowledge base of content and child development.

Accomplished teaching means planning and demonstrating effective instruction for *these students, at this time, in this place.* The National Board describes accomplished teaching practices in the Standards developed for each certificate. They are specific teaching behaviors that accomplished teachers demonstrate within their teaching practice. As a candidate for National Board Certification, you will show evidence of the Standards in your teaching practice.

THE ARCHITECTURE OF ACCOMPLISHED TEACHING

The Architecture of Accomplished Teaching (AAT) is a double helix representation of accomplished teaching practice as it applies to the lessons candidates use in their entries and in assessment center exercises. It is designed to give a visual of how the accomplished teaching of units of study and lessons are organized. It is an under-used tool that can add greatly to the understanding of the National Board process and what the National Board is looking for. Candidates often lament that if they just knew what the National Board wanted, they'd know what to do for each entry. In truth, candidates who understand the AAT and use its structure as the basis for planning their lesson sequences will demonstrate what the assessors want—evidence of accomplished teaching. This tool is found in your *Portfolio Instructions Part 1*. Keep a copy near your computer for frequent and easy reference.

What Works: Studying the Architecture of Accomplished Teaching

Step 1 —Start with knowledge of your students *(Proposition 1)*

- Who are they? Where are they now in their learning? Where should you begin?
- What knowledge about your students influenced the goals you set?
- How do you incorporate this knowledge into your lesson planning?

Step 2 —Continue setting high, worthwhile goals *(Proposition 1)*

- How do the goals you set connect to your Standards and portfolio instructions?
- How do the goals fit in the sequence of your overarching goals?
- What do you want your students to know at the end of the lesson or unit?

Step 3 —Implement instruction *(Proposition 2)*

- What approaches do you plan to use to accomplish your goals?
- In what sequence might you plan the strategies you plan to use?
- How will the strategies you choose support your students' learning?
- What is your rationale for implementing instruction this way?
- What criteria might you use to decide if and when to use another strategy?

Step 4 —Evaluate student learning *(Proposition 3)*

- How will you assess student learning?
- Why did you choose these methods for these students at this time, in this setting?
- What evidence will let you know that the instruction was successful—or not?
- What, if anything, did the assessment(s) tell you about your instruction?
- Where will you go next?

Step 5—Reflect on the effectiveness of your lesson design and decisions *(Proposition 4)*

- How do you know whether you made the right choices?
- What was successful and what was not?
- How could students reflect on their own learning?

Step 6—Set new, high, worthwhile goals *(Proposition 4)*

- How will you decide when it is time to move on in the lesson sequence?
- What indicators will you use to set new goals?

SSTARS: Here Is an Acronym to Jog Your Memory about the AAT

- Students: Know your students and how they learn. Proposition 1
- Set high, worthwhile, and appropriate goals. Propositions 1 and 2
- Teach using appropriate, effective strategies. Propositions 2 and 3
- Assess student progress using a variety of evaluation types and forms. Proposition 3
- Reflect on your teaching and your students' progress. Proposition 4
- Start the process again.
- See Appendix Figure 2.1 for a lesson plan template that uses SSTARS.

Why It Works

The elements of the AAT provide a complete lesson or unit plan that will have the greatest impact on student learning.

What Works: Knowing When to Use the Writing Styles

- Use mainly *descriptive* writing with some analysis for Steps 1, 2, and 3.
- Use mainly *analytical* writing for Step 4.
- Use mainly *analytical and reflective* writing for Steps 5 and 6.

Why It Works

Use the AAT to discern the nuances in the prompts. This will help you use the appropriate writing style for each. The prompts align with the Architecture's steps, and using it will help you find evidence of your thinking and teaching to write about.

THE SCORING RUBRICS AND EVALUATION OF EVIDENCE GUIDE

The scoring rubrics found in the *Scoring Guide* and *Evaluation of Evidence Guide* are also under-utilized resources that can be life-savers. Both are found in the "Scoring" section of the "Candidate Center" tab on the NBPTS website homepage. These are the documents that assessors have beside them as they score. How your entry will be scored is not a secret! Everything you need to show evidence of is listed in a user-friendly bullet format in the scoring rubrics and the headings in the evaluation guide.

What Works: Studying the Rubrics

- Read all of the levels from Level 4 down to Level 1. You will see a great difference in the quality of evidence present in each one.
- Concentrate on the Level 4 rubric. Keep it beside you as you write so that you'll know exactly what evidence you need to show. Be sure you have evidence for each bullet. Notice how it aligns with parts of the AAT. Use the Level 4 rubric to self-assess each entry. Go

through it bullet by bullet to be sure you've included everything you need. If something is missing—put it in!

WHAT WORKS: INCLUDING THE 3 CS OF EVIDENCE

- *Clear:* Anyone who reads your written commentary should be able to understand what you are saying. You've explained acronyms and educational terms. The sequence of events can be easily followed. Your writing is readable and makes sense.
- *Consistent:* Your writing needs an element of continuity. Don't say one thing in the first paragraph and then contradict it later. Numbers must add up, time lines need to be accurate, and your data must be shared honestly.
- *Convincing:* Present the case that you are an accomplished teacher. This means you present your evidence, and it is believable and achievable. The best way to do this is to include specific examples, documentation, and verification. Including specific examples provides stronger, more convincing evidence.

Here's Why It Works

Using effective tools such as the AAT, the scoring rubrics, and the *Evaluation of Evidence Guide* will make the process less frustrating and more meaningful because you'll know where to go for guidance and clarification. Make these tools work for you!

CANDIDATE VIGNETTES

Follow three candidates through their journey to National Board Certification. Lynn, Rick, and Jan aren't their real names, but everything else is real and actually happened to candidates I've known or worked with. You may find yourself in situations similar to the ones these fictional candidates experienced. For sure you'll recognize the feelings, emotions, frustrations, and triumphs they experience. They are all excited but don't really know what to expect or what lies ahead. Which candidate(s) will you most identify with?

August: Gearing Up

Lynn

Lynn spent the summer reading her Portfolio Instructions, Standards, and other National Board documents. She started working on Entry 4 but hasn't gotten very far because she was away on vacation for several weeks. She's organized her National Board binder and folders for each entry. Her principal has asked her to serve on three committees this year and she's her department chairperson. She's heard that the National Board process takes a lot of time, so she's trying to get off one of the committees. When she attends her first NB Cohort meeting, she works with colleagues to map out a time line to follow.

Rick

Rick considers himself a better-than-average teacher and doesn't think putting together his National Board entries will be very hard. He got his master's degree recently and dashed off most of the required papers and projects in pretty short order. He's made a list of possible accomplishments for Entry 4, and although, through his coaching duties, he communicates with families, he realizes that parent/community interactions are lacking within his school teaching load. He makes a note to look for ways to boost those communications for the coming year. But how hard can Entry 4 be with only 3 questions to answer for each accomplishment?

Jan

Jan spends many hours reading her certificate Standards and trying to digest all the National Board documents that are available to help her. But rather than feeling helped, she feels overwhelmed. She began work on Entry 4 during the summer and brainstormed possible activities to use as accomplishments, but now needs to narrow the list. She's having a hard time deciding which activities might be strong enough to use and what documentation she could provide for the ones she chooses. She is also trying to decide which entry to try and do first with her class. What seemed exciting back in the spring now seems daunting.

Chapter Three

Getting Started and Getting Support

Six Word Memoir: Start sooner—NOW—rather than later! —Lynn, AZ

LEARNING THE STANDARDS, THE LINGO, AND THE ENTRY REQUIREMENTS

New candidates often don't know where to start. They know they're embarking on a unique journey but aren't sure what steps to take first. If this describes you, read on.

- Refresh your understanding of the Five Core Propositions. They are the umbrella under which all other National Board documents are organized.
- Read and internalize the standards for your certificate. You must know what they look like in practice and how you use them in your practice.
- Read your *General Portfolio Instructions, Part 1*. This is an under-utilized resource with a wealth of information that is easy to refer to later.
- Study the *Learning Portfolio-Related Terms* (glossary) section in the General Portfolio Instructions, Part 1 to become familiar with National Board "language" that is specialized and specific to the National Board process. Certain phrases are used repeatedly in your instructions, and the glossary is where they are defined.
- Familiarize yourself with the *Entry Overviews* at the beginning of your Portfolio Instructions to understand the content of each entry.
- Study the *What Do I Need to Do?* section of each entry for a list of entry requirements.

WHAT WORKS

Familiarize yourself with the Portfolio Instructions, National Board language, and structure of the entry to get the big picture and the tools and confidence to move forward.

NAVIGATING THE NATIONAL BOARD WEBSITE

The National Board website, located at www.nbpts.org, contains a wealth of information. Everything you want and need to know to complete your portfolio and assessment center exercise is there. This is a complex site and, although recently redesigned, not always easy to navigate. For the purposes of this chapter, I will assume that everyone reading this is already a candidate, so I'll highlight the areas a candidate needs most. Take time to look at all the tabs found on the homepage, but here is a guide to the major sections and documents you'll use most. On the Homepage, you'll most often use the *Candidate Center Heading.* Click on *National Board Candidates*—the section you'll need most often. Click on *Certificate Areas* and you'll find every certificate available.

- **Certificate Areas**. Scroll down and click on your certificate. This new page is loaded with information and the documents you'll go to frequently: (1) a "nutshell" of the certificate, (2) a Notice of Revision if applicable, (3) the Assessment at a Glance document, (4) the standards for your certificate, (5) the Portfolio Instructions (Parts 1 and 2), and (6) the Scoring Guide (Parts 1 and 2 and the Evaluation of Evidence Guide).
- **Assessment at a Glance.** This is a comprehensive overview document that contains a wealth of information regarding the portfolio entries, your Standards, the Assessment Center (AC) exercises including AC exercise descriptions, two retired prompts, and the scoring process.
- **The Standards.** The Standards are the National Board's "bible" for describing accomplished teaching, and candidates are expected to show that they apply the Standards in their teaching practice. This document is comprehensive in its scope and contains many examples of accomplished teaching in each Standard. You will refer to the Standards repeatedly as you write your Written Commentary for each entry. Be sure to download and print this document for frequent reference.
- **Portfolio Instructions.** The first link takes you to your complete set of instructions for the four entries and includes all the forms you'll fill out and submit. Some certificate areas also have an appendix with specialized content-area information that will be important to access as you plan and write your entries. The *General Portfolio Instructions,* which are the same for all certificates, contain information pertinent to all certificate areas regarding preparation, development, and the submission of your entries. Here is where the Architecture of Accomplished Teaching, a glossary of terms, and writing samples are found.
- **Scoring Guide.** Scroll down and you'll find links to *Part 1, Part 2,* and the *Evaluation of Evidence Guide. Part 1* gives general information about all aspects of the scoring process, how the scores are connected to the Five Core Propositions, information about the assessors, explanations of the feedback comments given on any entry that scores less than 3.75, and retaking an entry. *Part 2* gives the scoring rubrics for each entry *and* the six AC exercises in your certificate. Whenever someone suggests "looking at the rubric" for an entry or exercise, this is the document and information they are referring to. Assessors use the Level 4 rubric to assess your entry and AC exercises. It's no secret what the assessors are looking for—it's all in this document. *The Evaluation of Evidence Guide* is the document assessors have beside them as they score.
- **Frequently Asked Questions (FAQs).** At the time of this writing, the FAQ section is under construction on the website. Once developed, it will be a place to go for quick answers to many details you'll have questions about.

What Works

Being familiar with the documents and resources you need to complete your portfolio and prepare for the Assessment Center exercises will save you time and grief!

Why It Works

Knowing where to go quickly for information is one way to work smart!

ORGANIZING YOUR NATIONAL BOARD MATERIALS

Once you have a basic overview of the portfolio, it's time to implement some organizational strategies to help keep the myriad of written commentary drafts, paper piles, and artifacts you'll assemble. Here are several systems candidates have used successfully. Pick one or a combination that suits your own style and work habits.

What Works: Organizing KISS Options (Keep It Super Simple!)

- Spiral-bind each set of entry instructions. You'll end up with four "books" that are easy to carry for reference. They are also sturdy and will stand up to heavy use. Your school may have a machine that does this operation, or go to an office supply store.
- Keep instructions in a binder sectioned for each entry. On the plus side, this keeps all instructions in one place. But binders can be heavy and awkward to carry, and pages can tear away from the rings. Still, it's a familiar organizational system for many candidates.
- Use a file box with sections or hanging folders for each entry and for student work.
- Create a file folder resource for *each entry* to hold your written drafts. Here's how:

    1. Lay a file folder in front of you, closed like a book.
    2. *Front cover:* Copy, cut, and paste the first page of your entry instructions that includes the *Standards* and the *Accomplished Teachers* bullets. Shrink as needed to fit.
    3. *Inside Left:* Open the folder. Copy, cut, and paste the *Level 4 rubric* for this entry found in the Scoring Guide.
    4. *Inside Right:* Copy, cut, and paste the *Composing Written Commentary* prompts.
    5. *Back Cover:* Draw a T-chart listing the Standards and examples from your practice.

Laminate the folder for durability. Do this for each entry. You won't believe how handy this reference is! Later, when you ask someone for feedback on your writing, put your draft in this folder. Your reader will have all the information needed to know the entry requirements.

Why It Works

Following a *KISS* system will be a lifesaver. You won't stress over time you wasted hunting for work and documents. Designate a place for your work—and keep it there!

ORGANIZING YOUR WRITTEN COMMENTARY ON YOUR COMPUTER

- Get comfortable with your computer—it will become your best friend.
- Use a reliable word processing program.
- Follow all instructions as to font, type size, line spacing, margins, headers, footers, and page numbers. Format each entry the first time you write.
- Label each draft with the date. This will ensure you are working on the latest version.
- Create a folder for each entry, and save drafts in their appropriate place.
- As you start to write each entry, type all the prompts in a color. This will ensure you don't skip any prompt. As you get close to finishing, shrink the size of the colored prompts. This will help you estimate the length of the entry.

- Periodically print out drafts or back them up on a CD or flash drive/memory stick you can use on any computer. This step will save you a lot of stress if your computer crashes or your laptop is lost or stolen.
- As you choose student work samples, instructional materials, and documentation for Entry 4, scan them into your computer to have them ready for e-submission.
- Remember: save early, save often and save everything! Back up your files frequently.

Doing everything you can to keep your writing accessible and safe is prudent and smart. Nothing is worse than losing what you've worked so hard to produce!

ORGANIZING YOUR TIME

Figuring out how to organize your time is by far the most difficult challenge. As you well know, teachers are incredibly busy both at work and at home. Family and work continually compete for your time and energy. Here are some strategies successful candidates have used to help them cope with the time demands that National Board Certification places on them:

- *Just for this school year* say no! Eliminate as many committees and school responsibilities as possible. Promise your principal that you'll be back next year.
- *Just for this school year* say no at home too. Delegate chores and activities. This is not the year to become team parent for all of your kids' sports teams and activities. Resign if you already are—spread the joy and let some other mom or dad take a turn.
- Set aside a designated daily or weekly work and writing period. Some candidates arrange for their spouse to be in charge of the family on Saturday or Sunday afternoon or for one weeknight. Other candidates stay late at school once a week or go to their classroom to work on the weekend. This is especially important from January to your deadline date.
- Consider arranging a weekend away from home so you can work undisturbed. Go to a hotel or a cabin or housesit for a friend who is away—anywhere you can be alone—or send your family away!
- Create a flexible and realistic time line and do your best to stick to it.
- Recognize that from March through May you'll need additional time to finish and polish entries.

What Works

- **Avoid procrastination** . It will come back to haunt you. Some candidates say they work better under pressure, and that may be true *for a few*. But in the National Board process you can't quickly dash off a paper and produce a quality portfolio. The portfolio requires a great quantity of quality evidence collected over time, and putting together a successful portfolio is too complex to be done in a hurry.
- **Be aware** that you will need to work on more than one entry at a time.
- **Look at** your academic scope and sequence and begin to map out units for your entries.
- **Look at** each entry and earmark lessons you teach that will fulfill the requirements.
- **Start researching** if you need to show something you aren't familiar with. For example, early and middle childhood generalists have a science/math entry that requires inquiry science. If inquiry science is unfamiliar to you, then you will need to learn about it.

- **Start early and save everything.** Save student work. Save evidence of anything that could be used for Entry 4. Save "out-takes" of your writing you cut when editing. You never know when a phrase or idea you cut could be used.

Why It Works

Organizing your time wisely can be a make-or-break factor in the quality of your portfolio. Organization will help you finish on time and produce quality work.

BUILD A SUPPORT SYSTEM: COHORT SUPPORT

When National Board Certification began, candidates were few and far between—both in numbers and location. It wasn't unusual for someone to be the only candidate in his or her entire state. Fortunately, few candidates face that kind of isolation today. Thanks to already certified National Board Certified Teachers (NBCTs), a continuum of support has developed across the country. Candidate support systems may be available in or near your school district.

If you are in a cohort, you will work with a candidate support provider (CSP) or facilitator who will guide your group and be obligated to provide and uphold ethical candidate support according to NBPTS guidelines.

CSP Responsibilities

- Help candidates understand the instructions and process more clearly.
- Help candidates think more clearly and deeply about their teaching practice.
- Help candidates learn to analyze the evidence presented.
- Help candidates engage in self-evaluation.
- Offer patience and encouragement.
- Guide candidates towards making their own decisions about evidence.
- Meet regularly with the candidate cohort and encourage peer collaboration.
- Share knowledge, skills, and experiences.
- Listen nonjudgmentally.
- Ask probing questions.
- Maintain confidentiality.

What CSPs Cannot Do

- Guarantee a certifying score.
- Tell candidates their writing is wrong, flawed, not good enough, or that an entry will or will not score well.
- Make a judgment call about portfolio instructions that seem unclear.
- Share NBCT portfolios or videos as teaching examples or tools.
- "Make" candidates into accomplished teachers or an NBCT.
- Create evidence for candidates or tell them how to write the Written Commentary.
- Tell candidates which students to feature, which student work to submit, which videos to submit, or which segment of a video "will work" for sure.
- How to revise, edit, or fix an entry.

If you participate in a cohort, you have responsibilities too—both to yourself and to the group.

Candidates Responsibilities

- Make an investment in time and attend scheduled meetings.
- Share fears, concerns, and issues.
- Continually read, review, and apply the standards.
- Bring work and questions to sessions.
- Keep to established time lines.
- Accept feedback in a professional manner.
- Study the portfolio instructions.
- Come to meetings prepared.
- Maintain confidentiality.
- Commit time to the process.
- Celebrate steps along the way.

What Works!

If you don't have a cohort, you can still find support. Try these ideas:

- Form your own cohort. If there are other candidates in your district or area, organize a monthly meeting. Consider rotating the location so that all candidates host the group.
- Meet with other candidates outside your regular cohort meeting dates.
- Find online support. There are a number of National Board support groups on Yahoo, on Facebook, and on the NBPTS website. See chapter 11 for an extensive list of support sites.

Why It Works

Collaborating with others gives you a sounding board and a place to ask questions and hear others' perspectives. Getting organized with a system that is user friendly may take some trial and error. Once you find one that works for you, you'll feel more secure about moving forward.

CANDIDATE VIGNETTES

October: Keeping It Together

Lynn

Lynn used a folder system for each entry. In each folder she put a copy of the entry instructions and anything she needed to collect for it. She tried to make a manageable time line for completing each entry. She planned Entry 1 and collected lots of student work. She started thinking about the video entries but thought the units of study that would be best are ones she teaches later in the year. She wrote the instructional context for Entry 1. She put all the other entries on the back burner so she could finish Entry 1.

Rick

Rick preferred keeping the entries and his standards in a large binder. He kept student work separate in a large folder and planned to take photos over the next few months of projects that wouldn't fit in the box. He didn't feel he needed to plan a time line because he is usually pretty organized and has always been able to complete writing assignments for college papers easily.

He started working on Entry 1, but responding to the questions took more time and thought than he anticipated. The assignments he liked best didn't seem to fit the entry prompts very well, but he decided to use them anyway. Eventually he had to scrap those assignments and teach another series of lessons. They fit the prompts better, and he collected student work from all students.

Jan

Jan kept everything in her box because she wanted everything in one place. It started to fill up pretty quickly, so she found a bigger box to use. She continued working on Entry 4. It took much longer than she thought it would, but she wanted to finish Entry 4 before starting on another entry. She realized that she needed to use accomplishments other than the committees she served on, so she started a new list of other activities.

Chapter Four

The Reflective Teacher, Metacognition, and the National Board Process

Six Word Memoir: Reflecting on teaching brings enlightening insight. —Annie, NM

In the 1930s education philosopher and reformer John Dewey wrote his explanation of *reflection* and its use in education. He wrote that reflection is a skill different from and more rigorous than other forms of thought. He described a specific mind-set conducive to reflection: a reflective teacher is confident about his or her practice and abilities as a professional but is willing to take action when evidence of needed change is identified and is able to consider new ideas, alternative actions, and other points of view.

Metacognition, a term first used in 1979 by Stanford University professor emeritus and clinical psychologist J. H. Flavell, is the skill of thinking about thinking. It revolves around one's knowledge about one's own "knowing": "noticing or identifying" something and then acting on that knowledge—in other words, analyzing and reflecting.

Two particular kinds of teaching competencies contribute to analytic expertise: (1) subject or content knowledge and (2) pedagogical knowledge. Subject knowledge relates to content—the *what* of teaching. Pedagogical knowledge is the art and craft of teaching—the *how* of teaching.

Within these competencies are five distinct yet interrelated skills:

- Setting learning goals
- Teaching the lesson or content in light of the goals
- Assessing whether goals are achieved
- Analyzing why the goals were or were not achieved
- Reflecting to revise the lesson or start over and set new learning goals

Reworded, these skills are the foundation of the *Architecture of Accomplished Teaching!*

Reflection is a special kind of self-analysis. In reflection, one looks back in order to look forward. One looks back, analyzes events or actions, then uses that analysis to make changes for the future. In order to reflect on and analyze the success of a lesson and make decisions as to whether any revisions are needed, one must look back and analyze each step. The National Board has incorporated the competencies of subject knowledge and pedagogical knowledge, as well as the related skills, into the National Board process.

- They are embedded into the Five Core Propositions and the Standards for each certificate.
- They mirror five of the six steps in the Architecture of Accomplished Teaching.
- They are the basis for many prompts throughout the entries and modules.

Most teachers are reflective by nature. But the National Board Certification process requires reflection to a greater degree. Never before have you scrutinized your practice with such a fine-tooth comb. Never have you looked at your students and your instructional decisions under a magnifying glass of such magnitude. The challenge is to get your thinking onto paper in a clear, consistent, and convincing way.

What Works

Put your reflection skills to work on these questions about your lessons that are connected to the competencies and skills:

- What, specifically, were students to learn or be able to do during the lesson sequence?
- Is your content knowledge current and accurate?
- Did you competently convey this knowledge within the lesson?
- Were the goals appropriate? Why? How do you know?
- What strategies and activities did you use to teach the lesson?
- Why did you make those pedagogical decisions?
- What would evidence of learning look like?
- How do you know the learning did or did not take place?
- How did you assess the learning?
- Was the assessment directly tied to the learning goal? Did the assessment "match up" with the goal?
- What student actions or conversations provide evidence they did or did not learn the goal?
- What teacher actions led to students' learning (or not learning) the goal?
- What other factors influenced the learning?
- When you look back and analyze the goal setting, teaching, and assessment, what evidence connects the student learning to your instruction?
- What proof do you have that the learning connects to your teaching practice?
- How did your instructional choices factor into the learning that did or did not take place?
- How might revisions in your lesson planning or implementation result in improvement?
- What revisions would you consider?
- How and why might those revisions result in a better outcome?

Why It Works

Such questions are the essence of many of the prompts in Entries 1, 2, and 3. Your ability to engage in metacognition to describe, analyze, and reflect on the competencies demonstrated in your teaching practice will determine the outcome of your efforts to become a National Board Certified Teacher (NBCT).

CANDIDATE VIGNETTES

October: Stalemate

Lynn

Lynn is close to being back on track with the time line she developed in August. She's gotten a video for Entry 2 and is planning lessons for Entry 3. While rereading the Entry 3 Standards, she has an "aha" moment and realizes the prompts tend to follow the Architecture of Accomplished Teaching, so she looks that graphic over too. All of October is spent getting a video for Entry 3. She takes her videos to her cohort meeting for feedback. Her cohort thinks the Entry 3 video is stronger than the Entry 2 video, so she considers filming Entry 2 again. She realizes the video lacks evidence for two standards. She starts writing Entry 3 on her fall break.

Rick

When his CSP asks candidates to share their progress, Rick doesn't volunteer any information. He's supposed to have an Instructional Context (IC) ready, but he doesn't have any writing yet. When the CSP talks with Rick, rather than explaining his practice, he tends to argue and give excuses why he has nothing written yet. His coaching season is just getting into full swing; one of the students he planned to use for the Entry 1 moved away; and on and on. The writing doesn't seem very hard—he just hasn't gotten to it yet. The CSP questions almost everything the candidates share, but he listens and makes some notes to use later.

Jan

Jan feels ready to quit. She isn't ordinarily a quitter—in fact she's the go-to person at school to get things done. That's the problem: she has so many other obligations she can't seem to get any National Board work done. She hasn't accomplished nearly what she thought she would by now and feels behind. She has meetings two and three days almost every week plus her reading endorsement classes. She passed on being team mom and found someone to share teaching the church class, which has helped a little. The whole National Board commitment now seems so big she doesn't see how she can do it all. She is supposed to have an IC written to share at her cohort meeting, but she hasn't been able to decide which entry she wants to work on first, so she is empty handed. If something doesn't change soon, she feels she may need to withdraw.

Chapter Five

Writing for the National Board

Six Word Memoir: Abandon beautiful wordage: Clear, Consistent, Convincing. —Kristin, AR

PRESENT YOUR CASE

Writing National Board entries is unlike any other kind of writing you've done. It's not like the creative writing assignments you did in high school or college. It's not even like writing a term paper or master's thesis. Your score isn't determined by your grammar or sentence structure, fancy language, or the number of research citations you include. In fact, some attributes of what is typically considered good writing don't necessarily apply here. So, what is it like?

Writing for the National Board is, above all else, *evidentiary,* meaning written to present *evidence.* Your sole purpose is to present evidence of your accomplished teaching, learning, leadership, and collaboration. It isn't quite as easy as pie, but it isn't rocket science either.

You must make a case for your accomplished teaching the same way a lawyer argues a case in the courtroom—by presenting strong *evidence.* You are the defendant acting as your own attorney, presenting evidence of what you do in your classroom. Your student work samples, videos, and responses to the prompts are the evidence of your accomplished teaching. The assessor is the judge and jury.

OVERVIEW OF THE THREE STYLES OF WRITING: DESCRIPTION, ANALYSIS, AND REFLECTION

Just as an attorney uses questioning styles to elicit evidence, the National Board uses writing styles that can be explained in three verbs: *describe, analyze,* and *reflect.* Each prompt connects to one or more writing style to help you present information that is *clear, consistent,* and *convincing. Describe, analyze,* and *reflect* are verbs that tell what you must *do.* The noun forms, *description, analysis,* and *reflection,* are the *results* of your actions.

DESCRIPTION TELLS "WHAT"

When you describe something, you tell *about* it; you tell *what* occurred. In court, a witness gives the facts in order to paint a clear picture of a situation. There should be no interpretation

23

or judgment in descriptive writing. In a National Board entry, you respond with enough information for the assessor to form a picture or impression of what you want to depict. Key words in prompts that ask for description include the following:

Tell   Explain   List   Describe   What

A descriptive passage:

- Tells or retells the main facts.
- Is logically ordered.
- Has enough detail to set the scene and give assessors a basic sense of the class, student, or situation you need to describe.
- Contains accurate, precise enumeration where appropriate.
- Includes elements and features that allow an assessor to "see what you see."
- May be used in conjunction with analysis. You often need to describe the subject or situation you are analyzing so that it is visible to the assessor, making the analysis more meaningful. But the borders between them can be fuzzy.

Description in the Entries

Description is the easiest type of writing to do. Most teachers find description easy to write and typically tend to describe way too much. Although it is important to use description to give the facts and paint a picture of your class, students, and activities, it isn't the most important type of writing. Why? *It is the least evidentiary of the writing styles.* Description sets the tone, draws a picture, and gives the facts. But it doesn't deliver much, if any, evidence. That is the task of analysis and reflection.

The *Instructional Context* sections of Entries 1, 2, and 3 are the largest descriptive passages you will write. These sections give assessors a sense of your teaching context and the featured class and student(s). Tell enough to give the assessors a realistic picture of the characteristics that shape your teaching and the personality of the class. Be sure to respond to every part of each prompt, but keep as close to page suggestion as possible (one page in most certificates) because you'll need space later for other, more evidence-rich sections of the entries. Here are some *hypothetical* descriptive passages that might be found in an Instructional Context:

- The featured class consists of 27 students, who are 11 to 14 years old. Science is the first period of the day. Several students are habitually tardy, which makes it difficult to begin instruction on time. Seven students are English language learners who leave 10 minutes early to go to the Resource Room for language instruction. Therefore I must complete the essential lesson elements before they go. *EA/Science*
- Jenny is both young and immature for a fourth grader. She reads on a second grade level and has particular trouble putting her thoughts on paper. She often misspells words and writes entire stories without using any punctuation. She likes to work with a partner but has difficulty staying focused on the task. *MC/Generalist*
- All students in this AP Statistics class plan to attend a four-year college. All students in the class have passed Algebra 2 and some are currently enrolled in Calculus 3. Nearly half of the students have taken an AP course before, but none have taken any statistics courses prior to this class. *AYA/Math*

- The learners in this computer class vary in their linguistic and academic abilities and state reading scores. The majority of students are in the "Basic" reading category which is below grade level. Four students are "Below Basic," which signifies they are far below grade level. Only one student in the whole class is "Proficient" and on grade level. The class personality is pleasant and cooperative, and most students are generally on task. *EA/YA/ Career and Technical Education*

Keep These Points in Mind When Describing

- Be succinct. Say enough to paint the picture, then stop.
- Decide which facts and details are significant, and emphasize those.
- Concentrate on facts and details that show an impact on teaching or learning.
- Resist the urge to tell *everything*. Details matter, but don't go on and on.
- Description should be the smallest portion of your writing.
- Follow suggested page limits. They are there for a reason—to keep you from writing too much description and not enough analysis and reflection.
- Support description with details and examples—but not too many.

ANALYSIS ASKS "SO WHAT?" AND "WHY?"

Description is the writing style that tells "what." Analysis is the writing style that asks "so what?" and "why?" Compare it to an attorney who puts forth a theory, then goes about confirming or rejecting it depending on the evidence. Teachers make hundreds of decisions each day that are implicit in their knowledge of their students and content area, but they seldom need to express this minutia orally or in writing. However, the analysis questions in each entry require this intrinsic knowledge be put into words on paper. Analytical writing is important because:

- It is the most evidentiary of the three styles.
- It demonstrates significance: *so what?* and *why?*
- It shows the assessor the reasons and motives (rationale) for your actions and decisions.
- It interprets and justifies actions and decisions—backed up with evidence.
- It shows the assessor the thought processes you used to reach decisions.
- It examines why elements or events are described in certain ways.
- It involves taking apart what occurred during a teaching event.

Prompts that ask for analysis may contain these key words:

How? Why? In what ways . . . Tell your rationale for . . . Explain why . . .

What Works: Use These Sentence Starters for Analytical Responses

- Because I know ___, I ___ (planned, provided, organized, taught . . .), which shows . . .
- I chose ___ because . . .
- There are several reasons why . . .
- The ___ on his paper showed me that he didn't understand ___, so I . . .
- The rationale behind my decision to ___ was . . .

- This was significant because . . .
- This impacted student learning by . . .
- Because ___, therefore . . .
- In order to ___, I . . .

The subject(s) being analyzed (student work samples or a video) must be available for the assessors. Clearly label your student work samples and/or video and refer to them in the text. Assessors will look at the student work samples and videos to compare them to the evidence in your analysis. Typically, the assessor reads your entry, looks at the work samples or video to see how they support your writing and "match up," and then reads the entry again. The analysis helps the assessors see the significance of the evidence you submit.

ASKS *NOW WHAT?*

The descriptive style of writing tells *what*—like a witness giving testimony, or a journalist. The analytical style asks *so what* and *why,* like an attorney questioning a witness or a scientist. The reflective style goes a step further and asks *now what?* Reflection is like a jury looking back at the evidence to decide a case or a follow-up visit to a doctor to monitor a course of treatment. Reflection is a kind of self-analysis that:

- Explains the thought processes used *after* teaching a lesson or unit.
- Tells how you would make decisions in the future.
- Is retrospective.
- Explains the significance of a decision.
- Tells the impact of a decision, activity, or action.
- Reviews instructional strategy choices.
- Sets new goals based on your analytical conclusions.
- Demonstrates your understanding of the National Board Standards.

Prompts that require reflection ask you to look back at your teaching practice and/or to look ahead and predict what you might do differently. Analysis and reflection often overlap. Reflective prompts may ask:

- What would you do differently if you were to teach the lesson again?
- What does the featured student's performance suggest about your teaching practice?
- Were these goals appropriate? Why?
- Were your lesson design, strategies, and materials appropriate? How do you know?
- How did students perform in light of the chosen goals?
- Could I have taken this a step further to increase student understanding?
- What did I learn from this experience that will help me do even better next time?
- What did I learn about my teaching practice in relation to student learning?

Reflection assumes that analysis has already taken place. A typical mistake teachers make is to retell rather than reflect. When you reflect you *explain* and *interpret* what happened, then tell what should come next. You look back, then forward.

Use These Pointers for Reflection

- *Be honest.* There is always something that can be done better. No lesson is perfect.
- *Be realistic.* Don't propose something that is clearly impossible.
- *Focus* on both strengths and weaknesses of a lesson. No lesson is a total failure.
- *Use* concrete evidence to support your statements.
- *Align* and connect your instructional goals, the assessment activity, and your reflection on the lesson. There must be total consistency and agreement among them.
- *Focus* on the impact your teaching had on your students.

What Works: Use These Sentence Starters for Reflective Responses

- In the future I . . .
- A key success was . . .
- An area for improvement is . . .
- My plan for the next lesson is . . .
- If I were to do this again . . .
- I learned ___, which will help me plan better next time by . . .
- Before this lesson my students . . . , but because of this experience . . .
- Because of this teaching experience I learned . . .

Why It Works

The boundaries between analysis and reflection are not clear cut. Analysis focuses on *so what;* reflection focuses on *now what?* Analysis is about the past; reflection is about using the past to determine future actions. Understanding reflection will make your writing stronger.

EVIDENCE OR LACK OF EVIDENCE IN YOUR WRITING

Read and reflect on the following samples to see if you can tell the difference in the amount of evidence presented in each pair of examples:

- *#1. With Evidence.* To prepare the class for writing, I planned a reading comprehension activity. I directed students to read a text and answer questions about it. Rory was unable to write responses in complete sentences. And he also skipped questions. To determine Rory's reading level, I administered the DAP (Developmental Reading Assessment) and used informal assessments. I learned that he could answer questions orally but struggled to put his thoughts on paper. Rory shared that when he saw a list of questions he felt overwhelmed. To address this problem, I began having him use a graphic organizer I designed that allowed him to record information in shortened form . . .
- *#1. Lack of Evidence.* Rory had trouble writing complete responses to comprehension questions, so I gave him a graphic organizer to help him organize his thoughts and information.
- *#2. With Evidence.* I set up my science lab and centers to encourage easy access to all materials and to give adequate space for the inquiry activity. In the beginning of the video, Marci was easily able to retrieve from the supply bins the string and yardstick her group needed to measure the distance their car rolled off their ramp. She and her group also had space to place their ramp and have room for the car to roll. When the car came to a stop

after rolling down the ramp, they used the string to measure from the bottom of the ramp to the front end of the car. Then they laid the string on a yardstick to measure the distance in inches and feet. Sam measured first, laid his string on the yardstick, and declared the distance to be 3 feet. Lynn said, "That is a yard. Our car traveled a yard!" I asked the others in the group is they agreed. Marci replied, "Yes, 3 feet is the same as a yard." This showed me that everyone in that group understood the measuring equivalents.

- *#2. Lack of Evidence.* My classroom is set up so kids can get their own supplies. One student from each group got supplies for their group. Each group set up their ramp and started rolling their cars down it to see how far they would travel. Marci's group rolled a car down their ramp, and it traveled a yard. They knew this because they measured with their string and a yardstick.

- *#3: With Evidence.* I used a variety of authentic materials and realia for this lesson to provide a more concrete visual of the foreign country. My bulletin board was covered with a map of Mexico, pictures from a Costa Rican calendar, newspapers from Spain, posters from a travel company, photographs from books, and magazine ads promoting Panama as a tour destination.

- *#3: Lack of Evidence.* I used materials and realia from Mexico, Costa Rica, Spain, and Panama for this lesson to provide a more concrete visual of the foreign country.

What Works

Give specific examples in your Written Commentary to give a clear, consistent and convincing picture of your accomplished teaching. *Examples = Evidence.*

Why It Works

Examples build a strong wall of evidence!

DANGER: STYLE FAUX PAS AND PITFALLS

While learning to write with the three styles of writing, some writing hazards emerge. Watch out for these and avoid them.

Missing Person Alert

Q: What is missing from this hypothetical passage? The students were introduced to their new vocabulary by using flash cards. After practicing as a whole group, they were divided into study groups. First they were assigned jobs within the group. Each group was provided with a set of flashcards and a worksheet to reinforce their learning. After all of the groups finished, we discussed the words again. Then each was assigned words to use in a sentence and illustrate.

Q: What is wrong with the above passage? *A:* The teacher is missing! Nowhere in that passage is the teacher mentioned. Who is the teacher? Where is the teacher? When writing your entries, don't hide in the background or be invisible. You must put yourself in the picture—clearly, consistently, and convincingly. How do you do that?

How to fix it: I introduced students to their new vocabulary using flash cards. After practicing as a whole group, *I* divided into study groups. First *I* assigned jobs within the group. then *I* provided a set of flashcards and worksheet to reinforce their learning. After all of the groups finished, *I* led a discussion about the words and assigned words to use in a sentence and illustrate.

What Works: Making Yourself Visible within Your Writing

- Write in the first person. Use the pronoun *I* frequently. Candidates often feel that writing about themselves is bragging, and that feels uncomfortable. Put those feeling aside and use first-person pronouns in order to showcase your actions.
- Be careful with the pronoun *we*. It takes more space, but it is stronger to say *the students and I* rather than *we*. That way it's clear just who *we* are; *you* are in the picture.
- Use *we* sparingly. Use it once, then switch back to *I*.
- In Entry 4, when using *we* to show collaboration, use it once, then turn the focus to your own contribution and switch to *I* or *my: I* collaborated with my department to plan the science fair. *We* each had assigned roles. *My* role was to . . .
- Use the active voice because it is clearer, more direct, and more concise. Go back and look at the example passage. Not only is the teacher missing, the verbs are almost all written in the passive voice. Sentences using passive voice verbs are wordier, longer, and less clear than those using the active voice. The "fixed" example uses active-voice verbs.
- Use *helping verbs, by,* and *–ing* endings sparingly. For example, say*: I provided flashcards* instead of *Flashcards were provided* or *I was providing*. After writing a draft, go back and highlight each verb phrase with a helper and/or *–ing*. Then rewrite as many as possible in the active voice.

Look again at the rewritten passage with pronouns that put the teacher into the picture and with active voice verbs. Do you see the differences?

Why It Works

This passage is much stronger because the teacher is clearly in the picture and the active voice verbs show who performed the actions expressed. There are also details to demonstrate how this teacher's actions support the National Board Standards. This lets the assessor know who led the lesson and how the teacher produced learning.

More Writing Faux Pas and Pitfalls

- *Preaching from the Pulpit.* This occurs when the candidate uses the Written Commentary as a soapbox. Avoid inserting personal views and frustrations about teaching into the Written Commentary. It is a waste of words and space. In a nutshell, accomplished teachers are able to demonstrate accomplished teaching and student learning in spite of difficulties and obstacles. Assessors score only *evidence* of accomplished teaching, so it is important to use words and space to demonstrate your evidence.
- *The ESP Communicator.* When candidates don't explain their actions and decisions clearly, the assessor is left to connect the dots. Be careful not to assume that the reasons for choices are so obvious that no explanation is needed. Some candidates may be clear about what they *do,* but they may write ambiguously or not at all about the thinking processes that led them to a particular decision. This is a common pitfall, especially among more experienced candidates whose actions have become so intuitive and automatic that they no longer deliberately think about the reasons for their decisions. It may seem tedious or annoying to be pressed into the deeper thinking that the analysis and reflection sections require. But you

must explain the thinking and decision-making processes you applied to student work samples, videos, or other artifacts used in the entries. Never assume that an assessor will "see" evidence without an explanation. Explain your decisions and choices.

- *The Feelings Guru.* This candidate substitutes feelings for concrete evidence. Work to eliminate all *I believe, I feel, I tried,* and *I think* statements from your writing. Although teachers are very caring people, the National Board entries are not the place to lay out your personal teaching philosophy or beliefs. Statements such as *I believe all children can learn . . .* or *I feel that all students should . . .* , however true, are irrelevant to the process. The assessor looks for *evidence* of a teacher's effectiveness, but a teacher's philosophy is not a measureable piece of evidence. Assessors look for evidence in the form of specific examples, descriptions, analysis, reflection, and artifacts such as student work samples and videos. Avoid these pitfalls by returning to the trial lawyer analogy. You must present evidence clearly, convincingly, and consistently to the assessors who are the judge and jury.

- *Jargon* is the specialized language, words, and terms used within a profession. Use it sparingly. Too much educational jargon gets in the way of understanding. The best writing is plain, simple, easily understood language—the kind you use when you talk.

What Works: Using Strong Verbs, Strong Phrases, and Bloom's Taxonomy

Writing strong National Board entries does not require a fancy vocabulary. The assessors come from all 50 states, from big cities and small towns, and are teachers just like you. Ask yourself whether anyone, from anywhere, will understand what you wrote, and you'll be on the right track.

Strong verbs and phrases describe accomplished teaching actions and qualities that have meaning within the National Board Certification process. They are words that help you showcase your teaching practice as described in the Standards. They are, for the most part, plain, strong verbs and descriptive phrases. Using these verbs and phrases in your writing can lend clarity and strength to your descriptions, analyses, and reflections. But the criteria for using them are authenticity and honesty. They must have meaning within the context of your teaching practice. Here are some examples:

- *Strong Verbs.* I encouraged, developed, designed, guided, supported, organized, facilitated, chose, chose to, selected, challenged, provided, gave, taught, engaged, demonstrated, learned, modeled, measured, asked, practiced, assigned, performed, contributed, impacted, influenced, instructed, questioned.

- *Strong Phrases.* Students as risk-takers, ways of learning, learning community, life-long learner, build self-esteem, promote student understanding, appropriate assessment, constructive feedback, fairness, equity, goal related, integrated learning, behavior intervention, active engagement/listening, high expectations, insightful questions, meaningful, learning goals, outcome based, reluctant learner, on task, rich and in-depth, inclusion, productive classroom, cooperative groups, parent partnerships.

- *More Strong Phrases.* Community involvement, collaboration, diverse perspectives, beyond the classroom, high expectations, problem solving, real-world applications, rich variety of sources, student ownership, teacher as a learner, teaching strategies, unique learning needs, varied assessments, work collaboratively, standards based, content oriented, application, direct impact on student learning, I learned, I should have, now I understand, relevant characteristics, motivational.

- *Bloom's Taxonomy.* This is one of the best references for finding effective verbs that indicate levels of learning and for planning appropriate lessons. Here is a recap (from lowest to highest levels):

  Remembering. Define, memorize, record, identify, label, list, locate, match, name, recall, spell, tell, state, underline, recognize, repeat
- *Understanding.* Restate, discuss, describe, explain, express, identify, interpret, paraphrase, put in order, restate, retell, summarize, review
- *Applying.* Apply, conclude, construct, use, dramatize, illustrate, show, sketch, draw, give a new example, solve, operate, practice, translate
- *Analyzing.* Distinguish, analyze, differentiate, appraise, experiment, compare, contrast, diagram, debate, categorize, classify, dissect, infer
- *Evaluating.* Defend, judge, value, evaluate, support, argue, appraise
- *Creating.* assemble, construct, create, design, develop, formulate, write

Why It Works

These verbs provide evidence in your writing. They indicate your deliberate participation in the processes that make up accomplished teaching and are examples of the language used in the Standards that shows evidence of accomplished teaching.

Apply the litmus test to decide if something meets the criteria for being universally understood. There must be no confusion about the terms used in the Written Commentary. This is especially true for the names of programs or materials you or your school utilizes. Be sure to spell them out and give a brief explanation. Examples:

- Career Ladder, a pay-for-performance program . . .
- NCTM, the National Council of Teachers of Mathematics

What Works: Creating a Writing Framework

- Make the case that you are an accomplished teacher by showing evidence of exemplary teaching. You are the lawyer. The assessors are the judge and jury.
- Connect the three styles of writing to the prompts: description, analysis, and reflection.
- Keep description to a minimum. Description tells *what.*
- Analysis asks *so what?* and *why?* and is the most evidentiary type of writing.
- Reflection asks *now what?* and is a type of self-analysis.
- Provide concrete examples of your actions and decisions.
- Write in the first person as much as possible.
- Use strong verbs and the active voice.
- Avoid using large amounts of educational jargon.
- Use buzz verbs, buzz phrases, and Bloom's Taxonomy language where appropriate.
- Be authentic.

Why It Works

Your writing is the "legal brief" of your portfolio. It contains all the evidence to show the assessors that you are an accomplished teacher.

What Works: Following the Three Cs in the Level 4 Rubric

- Clear. Never assume anything and explain everything.
- Consistent. Goals, activities, assessments, and so forth must match up and be connected.
- Convincing. Build a wall of evidence with examples.

Add more Cs:

- Concise. Make your point and move on. Write short, to-the point sentences.
- Correct. Use correct grammar and punctuation so the assessor can focus on your content.
- Concrete. Evidence needs to be specific, real, and measureable, not vague and ambiguous.

Style Tips

- Limit bolding, underlining, and caps. A little goes a long way.
- Be as consistent as possible with verb tenses.
- Talk to the assessor, not at the assessor. The assessor is your audience.
- Write in your own voice. Don't lose yourself in the writing process.
- State the *significance* of events.
- Avoid acronyms unless you are sure the assessor will understand them or you can explain them.
- Streamline writing and cut the fluff. Edit! Edit! Edit numerous times!
- Avoid *helping verbs* and *–ing* forms of verbs wherever possible.

Be Sure To:

- Back up your writing on your computer often!
- Pay attention to page limits. The assessors stop reading when they reach the limit.
- Follow portfolio instructions exactly.
- Answer *all* parts of every question or prompt. Respond *to* the question, not *about* it.
- Show impact on student learning.
- Connect your teaching practice to the Standards.
- Study the Architecture of Accomplished Teaching for insight into the prompts.
- Give up stressing about the vagueness of the prompts. It will only drive you crazy.

Why It Works

Clear, consistent, convincing writing showcases your evidence.

CANDIDATE VIGNETTES

November: On a Roll

Lynn

Lynn is hammering out Entry 3, editing and revising the writing she started in October. Although Entry 2 and Entry 3 ask for different things, responding to the Entry 3 prompts helps her understand where she went wrong with the Entry 2 video. She is determined to have the Entry 2 video before Winter Break. Lynn takes writing to her cohort meeting for feedback.

Revisions are definitely needed, but she feels she's on the right track. Her committee meetings and department responsibilities continue to eat away at her National Board work time.

Rick

Entry 1 is still elusive for Rick. He's collected quite a bit of student work, but now it's piling up and he's confused about choosing the samples to use. The prompts seem vague, which makes choosing samples even harder. He teaches average and below-grade-level students, so there is plenty of room for growth, but he's struggling to find evidence for some of the prompts. He seems to be writing the same things for both sets of students. The CSP suggests choosing students with different learning issues, but he really wants to use Laura and Tom, who have similar problems. He knows his CSP might question him about this, so he keeps it to himself. Rick thinks this entry will be easier for those who teach higher-level students than it is for him. Some candidates share their writing with colleagues, but not Rick. He works alone during the meeting.

Jan

When she had nothing to share at the October meeting, Jan's CSP noticed and talked with her about her situation. Jan admitted she had too much on her plate and explained how it was impacting the amount of time she had for National Board work. When she reads the instructions for an entry, she feels bewildered and doesn't know where to start. The CSP makes some suggestions that Jan tries to put into practice. As her CSP suggests, Jan puts away Entry 4 and chooses another entry to work on. She also types the prompts into a document so she isn't looking at a blank page. Doing this helps her understand what she needs to show for each entry, and she can begin planning backwards to create lessons to show those things. She also responds to the prompts in the Instructional Context of Entry 3. Now she feels she's moving forward at last.

Chapter Six

Probing the Prompts

Six Word Memoir: I thought I already answered that! —Tamika, MS

THE STRUCTURE OF THE PROMPTS

Understanding the language and intent of the prompts can be a challenge. Candidates often feel they are answering the same thing multiple times, and the language often can be difficult to decipher. "If only I understood what they are asking!" is a candidate's lament. Each prompt is written to help you provide evidence of the Standards in your teaching practice, and here is a revelation—they generally follow the steps in the Architecture of Accomplished Teaching!

Notice that the directions for each section ask you to *address or respond to* the questions, *not answer* them. This is more than just a nuance of language; there is a very important distinction between the two terms. *Address and respond* mean to write what is true for you in your teaching context. *Answer* implies something more "black or white," right or wrong. The prompts allow for open-ended responses that fit your teaching context. So there isn't just one way to demonstrate accomplished teaching. The prompts don't dictate any particular teaching style.

THE INSTRUCTIONAL CONTEXT/STUDENT PROFILE

The Instructional Context/Student Profile sets the tone for the Written Commentary. You might compare it to the ambiance of a restaurant, which sets the scene for your dining experience. The writing style for this section in Entries 1, 2, and 3 is largely descriptive—you are painting the picture of your classroom context. Yours may ask for information about a class or about an individual, and the prompts may differ from certificate to certificate. Read *your* Instructional Context/Student Profile carefully.

Take the Prompts Apart

Sometimes it helps to break a prompt apart and analyze what it asks for. In most certificate areas, the prompts in the Instructional Context are similar across Entries 1, 2, and 3, so the following can serve as an example:

Prompt 1: School Setting

- My school (pre-school, elementary, middle/high, charter, rural, urban, suburban)
- Subject of the entry
- Number of students in the class you are using for this entry
- Ages of students in the class (must be within the age range allowed in your certificate)
- Grade(s) of students in this class.

Prompt 2

What are the relevant characteristics of the class that influence your instructional strategies: How do these characteristics affect your instructional choices and strategies as they relate to instruction of this subject?

What is meant by *relevant?* Synonyms include *pertinent, applicable, significant,* and *important.*

- Ethnic diversity
- Cultural diversity
- Linguistic diversity (students and/or parents)
- Range of abilities (reading/math levels, gifted/talented, receives remedial services, etc.)
- Personality of the class (competitive, cooperative, etc.)

Prompt 3

What are the relevant characteristics of students with exceptional needs that influenced your planning of this period of instruction? How do exceptional needs or abilities within your class influence the choices you made as you planned this unit of study?

- Range of abilities: lowest to highest
- Cognitive challenges: gifted students may be considered exceptional needs
- Social/behavioral challenges
- Attention issues
- Sensory issues
- Physical challenges

Prompt 4

What are the relevant features of your teaching context that influenced your selection of this period of instruction: the realities of your social/physical teaching context?

- Available resources (or lack of resources)
- Scheduling (pull-out periods, special classes, etc.)
- Room allocation (shared space, in a pod, in a portable structure away from the building)

Prompt 5

What are the particular instructional challenges this class represents for this lesson sequence?

- Students' skills and abilities
- Previous experiences and learning related to the topic

The relevant characteristics described in the Instructional Context/Student Profile should appear again in the Written Commentary. It's not enough just to *tell* the relevant characteristics. In the Written Commentary; you must show yourself *using your knowledge* of the characteristics you wrote about. You must connect them with evidence. If you can't, the characteristic may not be relevant enough to include at all.

Aligning the Instructional Context/Student Profile Responses to the Entry

You may not be able to write one Instructional Context/Student Profile and cut and paste it intact for the three entries that have this section. The "slant" of the Instructional Context varies for each entry because each needs to focus on a different class and/or subject area. The relevant characteristics of a science or social studies class might differ greatly from those of a writing group. Teachers who are departmentalized know that the personality and relevant characteristics of each period's class differ. The first class of the day can be very different from the last class of the day. Even within the same group of students in a self-contained classroom, the instructional challenges and class dynamics can vary from subject to subject. So each entry's Instructional Context must focus on the characteristics of each particular class or subject area.

For example, for the MCGen Entry 1 (Writing) Instructional Context, a relevant characteristic might be that several students have difficulty with the editing step of the writing process. But for the Entry 3 (Science and Math Integration) Instructional Context that information might not be relevant. For Entry 3, one might write that students arrived in fourth grade with little previous science instruction or that several students are in a pull-out math resource program.

Information in the Instructional Context/Student Profile needs to be connected to information in the Written Commentary. For example, if you state that you provide a slant board, special writing paper, or a software program to aid with writing, assessors would expect to find these accommodations referenced later in the Written Commentary.

THE PLANNING AND INSTRUCTION SECTION

If the Instructional Context/Student Profile is the ambiance of the entry, the Planning and Instruction section is the appetizer. Again, this section may have different names in different certificates. Here you:

- Present your plans, overall goals, and objectives for the lesson sequence.
- Explain the rationale for the choices you made.
- Show how the learning was meaningful.

A key understanding about the prompts in all sections of the Written Commentary is that they are connected to the Architecture of Accomplished Teaching (AAT). That means that they are also connected to the Core Propositions and the Standards. So prompts in the Planning and Instruction generally follow Steps 1–4 of the AAT. This isn't written in stone, but it's a pattern generally evident in Entries 1, 2, and 3. Steps 5 and 6 are found in the Reflection sections. For example, Prompt #5 in the Planning and Instruction section of MCGen Entry 2: Building a Classroom Community through Social Studies is:

> *What instructional resources/materials did you use during this unit? What was the rationale for using these resources/materials? Be sure to include specific examples of any math or science technology(ies) used that show you or your students interacting with these technology(ies). Explain how these materials demonstrate the integrations of mathematics and science.*

This prompt would largely fall on Step 3 of the AAT: Implement instruction designed to attain the goals (you set). Implementing instruction requires decisions about which resources and materials to use to teach the goals and objectives. But to choose the most effective resources and materials the teacher must have already set worthwhile goals and have knowledge of his or her students, their personalities, and how they work best. Choosing wisely also requires knowledge of curriculum to make the most effective choices to succeed in reaching the goal. Therefore a comprehensive response to Prompt #5 would provide evidence for Steps 1, 2, and 3 of the AAT, and thus several Standards and ultimately Propositions 1, 2, and 3. Entry 4 is organized differently and does not follow this structure.

ANALYSIS SECTION

The Instructional Context/Student Profile set the tone, like the ambiance in a restaurant. The Planning and Instruction was the appetizer. The Analysis of Students' Responses or Analysis of The Video Recording is the entrée, or main course of the entry. The prompts in these sections require both specific examples and references to the student work samples or the videos.

Analyzing the Prompts

Every certificate has this or a similar prompt in one or more entries:
   How do you ensure fairness, equity, and access for students in your class? Cite specific examples from the video recording.
   Break the prompt into its parts:

- Fairness: Assignment was appropriate for learning level; appropriate expectations
- Equity: Expected to be engaged and on task; choice built into lesson to address learning styles; varied time allocation to complete work; students get what they need to succeed
- Access: Opportunities to participate and learn; materials available and easily in reach; student can reach all resources from his wheelchair independently
- Accommodations: allocate varied amount of work times; accommodations available; preferential seating; buddy assigned to help
- Adjust instruction: adjust pacing of lesson; use variety of strategies
- Tell specifically when and how within the lesson these actions occurred
- Refer to your certificate Standard for additional examples

Fabricated EA/Science Video Example

When the video begins, students are finishing their construction of a variety of ramps based on previous learning about Newton's Laws of Motion *(*fairness)*. I formed groups to accommodate learning styles and personalities, and each group decided on the roles each member would have *(*equity, access)*. I gave each group choices in the materials to cover the surface of their ramp *(*equity)*. Group 3's materials and the ramp are on a table instead of the floor so that Tina, in a wheelchair, can easily participate. I provided a picture card illustrating the directions for Aiden, who is autistic, and his aide is available for help as needed *(*access, accommodations)*. Note: Eliminate * words in the final draft.

What Works

Dig below the surface of your students' work or the video to show your depth of understanding.

Answer *all* parts of every prompt. Respond *to* the prompt, not *about* it.

* Scrutinize the work samples and video to identify the students' strengths and difficulties.
* Write about specific strategies that resulted in learning and fostered the students' academic development.
* Tell how the information helped you move them forward intellectually.
* Tell how you promoted the students' personal responsibility for learning.

Why It Works

The Analysis section showcases your knowledge of teaching and learning by explaining your thinking—that you know what actions you took and what decisions you made to show accomplished teaching.

DIDN'T I JUST ANSWER THAT?

Candidates are often frustrated because it seems that the questions are redundant, and it can feel as if you are answering the same question again. But that isn't really the case. Following are two prompts found in the *AYA/English Language Arts* Entry 1 that sound much alike:

Analysis of Student Work: The Student as a Reader: What about the student as an individual provides insight into his/her work samples and your analysis of them?

Analysis of Student Work: The Student as a Writer: What about the student as an individual provides insight into his/her writing samples and your analysis of them?

Now consider these prompts from the *EMC/Literacy* Entry 2:

Planning and Instruction: How did you foster an environment that allows the student(s) to actively and purposefully construct meaning from reading? How did you ensure the student(s) had the opportunity to reach high standards and expectations?

Video Recording Analysis: In the first segment of the video recording, discuss how your classroom environment encourages reading development. Provide evidence of how your classroom resources appropriately reflect the needs and interests of your student(s). How was this reflected in the video recording? Cite specific examples in the video recording.

What Works!

Analyze what is alike and what is different in prompts that sound alike. In the AYA/ELA examples, the difference is that one prompt is about reading and the other is about writing. Since these are both literacy skills, there could be some overlap, but there should also be a clear difference. In the EMC/LRLA examples, both prompts are about the learning environment, but each prompt has a slightly different slant. Again, there may be some overlap, but the response should explain how the learning environment (which may be the same) addresses different needs and interests.

REFLECTION SECTION

You've experienced the ambiance (Instructional Context/Student Profile), sampled the appetizer (Planning and Instruction), and savored the main course (Analysis of Student Work or Video). Last is the dessert or aperitif: Reflection. It may have the fewest prompts, but what it lacks in numbers, it makes up for in the depth of thinking that thoughtful responses require. Reflection is actually a particular kind of analysis—self-analysis. Self-analysis is what the reflection prompts ask you to do. You have to look inward and backward for these responses, which, like all responses in the entry, show evidence of the Propositions and Standards. Here are three reflection questions from the *AYA/History-Social Studies* Entry 2:

How well did your students become involved in and understand the main points of your lesson? What is your evidence?

Again, break the prompt into parts and respond to each separately:

- Involvement: 100%? Somewhat? Mostly? Scale of 1–10?
- Understands the main points? 100%? Majority? Half? Some? Totally missed the mark?
- Evidence? Observation? Test score? Completed assignment? Discussion?

Be honest with this appraisal. Cite specific examples.

What, if anything would you do differently if you had the opportunity to teach this lesson again to these students? Why?

Look back to analyze the success of the lesson, then look ahead and tell what you could do differently that would address areas that you wish had been better. No lesson is perfect, so there are *always* areas that could be better. The assessors expect that you will want the next lesson to be even better.

What was a successful moment/aspect of this lesson on the video recording? Explain why it was successful. Cite evidence.

These could relate to instructional materials, effective use of time, discussion, group cooperation, or any number of other events in the video. They can be positive and/or negative. *Example: When I ___, I thought I was addressing a teachable moment. However, in retrospect, it derailed the students' train of thought and bogged the lesson down.*

What Works: Writing a Thoughtful Reflection

- *Be honest.* The assessors are teachers like you. They work with kids everyday too. Although the evidence in the Written Commentary will give them a good indication of the impact of the lesson sequence on the students' learning, let them know that you are aware of areas that could be improved. You tried your best, but if everything didn't work out quite the way you planned, just say so. Recognizing where improvement could happen provides evidence!
- *Write a meaningful reflection.* Refrain from saying that everything about the lesson went perfectly and you wouldn't change a thing. Most lessons are more like country songs— filled with ups and downs. There is always something that can be done better.

- *Write a balanced reflection.* Reflection isn't only about what went wrong or what you would change; talk about the positives too. Reflection should show that you think about all aspects of your lessons and their impact on student learning.

Why It Works

There is no perfect lesson. Each has its own strengths and weaknesses. Showing that you recognize them shows your depth of knowledge of your subject matter and pedagogy, and your ability to reflect on your practice.

CANDIDATE VIGNETTES

December: The Half-Way Point

Lynn

As luck would have it, Lynn has a difficult December. Her own children are sick, along with a large number of students, and Lynn comes down with a cold that won't go away. She misses three days of school—the days she had planned to video again for Entry 2. Because so many were absent, when she returns to school, she must review content materials before she can film. On top of that, there are school-wide assemblies that take her class time, final exams, and a workshop day when she is away. The filming just isn't working out, and Lynn gives up for now. She continues to polish Entry 3 and decides to take up Entry 4 again. Her plan for Winter Break is to finish Entries 3 and 4, plan again for the Entry 2 video, and start planning Entry 1.

Rick

Rick has kept a Communication Log and has been surprised how helpful it's been in documenting parent contacts. He sees that the contacts are weighted heavily with negative issues and wonders if he can also find some positives to communicate as well. Entry 1 finally starts "coming together" now that he has student work samples. Rick hopes to have at least one video completed by Winter Break, but his coaching duties and lack of time have conspired against him. He feels other candidates have it easy compared to him because they don't have as many commitments and they have higher level students. He makes a couple of "practice" videos for Entry 3 but has trouble getting the kids to be on task and interact with each other the way they need to. They don't seem to know how to have a discussion. He also discovers that he talks a lot more than he realized.

Jan

Jan finished the Instructional Context for Entry 3 and makes plans for lessons to film. But the filming proves difficult. It's hard to coordinate the timing with the teacher who volunteered to film for her. Her students keep acting up when the camera is on. There are also issues with the equipment: a cord came unplugged which means the film looks edited, and without an external microphone it's hard to hear student conversations. Eventually she decides to do the filming herself, and hand-carries the camera from group to group. She experiments with lessons not connected to the National Board entry—just for practice. After several attempts she gets some footage that seems promising. Now, if only she can find time over the Winter Break to actually view the film and choose a segment!

Chapter Seven

Writing about Student Work: Entry 1

Six Word Memoir: Work samples reveal my teaching's impact. —Doug, CA

THE STUDENT WORK ENTRY

All certificates contain an entry that centers on the analysis of student work samples. In the Music certificate, the student work entry takes the form of a video because of the performance nature of music. Other certificates ask for paper-and-pencil samples. For this entry, you *collect* student work samples from a series of lessons, then *describe, analyze,* and *reflect* on the work of one or more students using examples that show growth over time. The work samples are the evidence of the effectiveness of your planning and teaching, your understanding of the Architecture of Accomplished Teaching, and your ability to describe, analyze, and reflect on your teaching practice.

School districts currently require teachers to document student achievement primarily through standardized test scores. The NBPTS cares about student achievement but recognizes a variety of ways in addition to test scores that learning can be demonstrated. Here, your analysis of student work is important because it is the means by which you evaluate your students' learning and the effectiveness of your teaching. When grading, teachers usually look for evidence in student work that shows understanding of the content. But in the National Board process, the assessors go deeper. They look at your *analysis* of student work to see what *evidence and examples of effective teaching* it provides.

The measure of accomplished teaching is its capacity to impact student learning. Effective teaching means that, as a result of your teaching practice, student achievement improves. That is why you need to plan the lesson sequence and choose the students and work you feature in this entry very carefully. Effective teaching relies on the teacher's knowledge of students and subject matter and the ability to plan engaging, appropriate lessons for *these students, at this time, in this setting.*

What Works: Planning the Lesson Sequence with the End in Mind

Teaching a lesson, then crossing your fingers and hoping that the evidence the assessors expect to see is there is not the smartest plan. Your goal is to satisfy the Level 4 scoring rubric, and *planning backwards* is an effective strategy to use. By that I mean designing your lesson sequence to fit the entry rather than trying to make the entry fit your lessons. Like planning a trip, you must have the destination in mind in order to get there. Plan lessons that embed the evidence assessors expect to see into the lesson. This is not cheating; it is smart planning!

PLANNING A LESSON BACKWARDS

- Start with the evidence assessors expect to see. The Level 4 rubric in your *Scoring Guide* lays out the expectations.
- The 3 Cs of *clear, consistent,* and *convincing* in the rubric should become your mantra.
- Read the bulleted list on your Level 4 rubric. These items are the evidence you need in the lessons to demonstrate in your teaching practice.
- Include each bulleted piece of evidence in your lessons, and show in the Written Commentary how they are connected to your teaching and the student work.
- Planning backwards will ensure you've addressed the steps on the Architecture of Accomplished Teaching.

The way to show *clear, consistent,* and *convincing* evidence to the assessors is to use the student work samples to explain exactly what you did and why. The assessors have only your entry to look at. The samples and the Written Commentary are your only avenues of communication with the assessors.

What Works: Planning a Lesson Using the Level 4 Rubric

What might it look like to incorporate the Level 4 rubric evidence into the planning of your lessons? To illustrate a teacher's thinking process, using the Middle Childhood Generalist (MC Gen) rubric as an example, read the *hypothetical* notes a teacher might write when planning the student work entry to include the evidence from the rubric. *The Level 4 performance provides clear, consistent, and convincing evidence that the teacher recognizes students' individual learning differences and past experiences to set high, worthwhile, and appropriate goals for student learning and connects instruction to those goals.*

- I'll pre-assess or take a writing sample to determine where my students are in the writing process and then plan specific activities to address those needs.
- I'll plan differentiated writing experiences over a period of time that address the learning differences represented in my class.
- I'll plan narrative and expository prompts that my students will find interesting.
- I'll provide reference and vocabulary materials for my new English speakers.

Why It Works

You can see how much information about the teaching process is embedded in the notes—and how it references the Architecture of Accomplished Teaching and the Entry 1 Level 4 rubric. The Written Commentary needs to reveal the thinking that went into the planning of the lessons and the actions you took to put the ideas into practice. That provides strong evidence of the rubric.

One last point: did you notice how often the pronoun *I* and other first-person references such as *my* were used? Count them. First person is the strongest voice to use when explaining your teaching practice. Strong voice adds value to your writing.

What Works: Choosing Students to Feature

In all certificate areas, whether on paper or video:

- Choose students for whom there is something to say. Select students for whom your teaching has *clearly, consistently,* and *convincingly* made a difference.
- Select students through whom you can *clearly, consistently,* and *convincingly* show the range of your teaching abilities.
- Select students whose work allows you to *clearly, consistently,* and *convincingly* demonstrate the effectiveness of your teaching strategies through differentiation.

Why It Works

Selecting students for whom there is something to say allows you to showcase your knowledge of students, content, and pedagogy.

What Works: Choosing Work Samples to Feature

- Choose samples that demonstrate the effectiveness of your teaching strategies.
- Choose tasks worthy of your students' time and effort.
- Choose samples that support the goals and objectives of the lessons.
- Choose samples that show students improving their performance over time.
- Choose complex assignments that challenge students' thinking and show their learning across disciplines—toss most worksheets and multiple choice assessments.
- Choose assignments that feature open-ended questions or prompts. They are strong choices because they provide an avenue for creativity, critical thinking, and showing understanding. Most worksheets don't do that.
- Choose samples that allow students to demonstrate a range of understanding about the content.
- Choose samples that show progression of learning and progress over time.
- Choose samples with meaningful feedback from you beyond *good job* or grammar and spelling corrections. The feedback should show specific guidance that will help the student know how to improve next time. Examples: *You used commas correctly in this writing!* or *Remember to use commas with words in a series.*

Why It Works

Choosing work samples carefully allows you to showcase your strategies and accomplished teaching.

What Works

Save examples of the following:

- Evaluation rubrics—yours and student-made ones provide strong evidence of self-assessment and student engagement.
- Sets of work or copies (color copies if the originals must go home) from several students. This will give you the widest selection. Date all work.
- A variety of types of work that pertain to your lesson sequence.
- Save more than you think you will need in case a student moves away.

- Take photos of work samples that won't fit in the box.
- Make sure work samples and instructional materials follow the directions for the type of work the entry requires, for all specifications, and addresses the goals of the lessons.

Why It Works

These types of examples give you choice, showcase your thinking and your strategies and give evidence of your explicit instruction.

ANALYZING STUDENT WORK

Planning and teaching the lessons that produce the student work samples show evidence of four of the Five Core Propositions and the Standards. They show:

- Evidence of your knowledge of your students *(Proposition 1)*.
- Evidence of knowledge of your content area *(Proposition 2)*.
- Evidence that you think systematically about your practice *(Proposition 3)*.
- Evidence that you manage and monitor your students' learning *(Proposition 4)*.

Analyzing student work to the depth required for this entry is very different from typical day-to-day grading. Grading papers usually entails assigning a mark, score, or symbol such as smiley face or star, returning the paper, and going on to the next topic. But grading papers that way isn't really analysis. Think of analysis as *insight*—what you "see in" a student's work, what the work *tells* you about student learning. Analyzing means looking at student work in order to understand and improve it.

- Notice *how* students show they understand the learning goal.
- Notice *which skills* the student already knows.
- Notice *misconceptions* about the learning goal.
- Notice *mistakes* the student makes.
- Notice *indicators* that the activity was successful or not successful.
- Decide *what the student needs next* to achieve the learning goal.

What Works: Your Analysis of Work Samples Shows Accomplished Teaching

- Be specific when analyzing and writing about student work.
- Add details to your writing to show your understanding of a student's learning—or lack of learning. This is how assessors evaluate your level of knowledge. For example, saying that a student *can't subtract* really doesn't say much at all. Instead, show that you know *why* the student can't subtract. For example:

    - The student subtracts inaccurately over zeros.
    - The student has trouble borrowing from numbers larger than three digits.
    - The student makes errors because columns aren't aligned.
    - The student doesn't know the subtraction facts.

After you analyze for specificity, plan your instruction to include what the student needs next (flashcard drill, graph paper to align columns, manipulatives, etc.) to address the deficit. This demonstrates your knowledge of subject, how to teach it, and your Standards.

Why It Works

The kind of analysis teachers do every day connects to strong evidence of what accomplished teachers should know and be able to do and makes your thinking visible. You already know how to do this!

LOOKING FOR EVIDENCE IN STUDENT WORK

Why does the National Board have an entry based on student work? Through student work samples, the assessor can see how well you can address the steps on the *Architecture of Accomplished Teaching* and do the following:

- Set appropriate, high, worthwhile goals.
- Choose appropriate, engaging materials and activities that will move students toward achieving the goals.
- Plan and deliver effective instruction.
- Adjust goals and instruction based on student performance.
- Use analysis of student work to assess and plan the next learning steps and set new goals.

Imagine that you've planned and taught lessons about an important topic for your entry. You collected stacks of student work samples that support the goals and objectives and represent the activities and assessments you planned. You've chosen the student(s) for whom there is something to say, and their work samples and your notes are beside you at the computer. You are ready to tackle the prompts in the entry. You are ready to start writing. But where do you start?

WHAT EVIDENCE SHOWS

Start by locating the evidence in the body of work you've collected. Evidence is an example that supports something you assert to be true. Choose evidence along a continuum from weak to strong that is most convincing. Convincing evidence is specific examples that show:

- Students engaged with the lesson's goal(s).
- How the materials and activities you use help the student(s) in meeting the learning goal.
- How you manage and monitor student learning.
- How you modify and adjust instruction to meet student needs.
- How you assess student work in relation to the stated goal(s).
- How you use the analysis of student work to plan next steps.

WRITING ABOUT EVIDENCE IN STUDENT WORK

Respond to each prompt with information that is true for the featured student(s). Discuss your analysis of their work and cite specific examples that have led you to these conclusions. Break the prompts into parts, paying particular attention to the *verbs,* such as *describe, cite,* or *explain,* that will clarify what *you do* or the *student does.* Pay attention to the *nouns* you are asked to address. These might include behaviors, evidence, or patterns. Consider this fabricated example from the AYA/ELA certificate and look for specific evidence: *To help Student A expand her reading repertoire, I provided a variety of texts including art magazines, dramatic presentations, cartoons, movies, TV shows, novels, Twitter feeds, and editorials, which resulted in her identifying that reading can take multiple forms and she can find texts that suit and expand her outside interests. She used to think that reading was a chore and read only what was required for school. But now she often shares in her journal what she's reading about and comments on what she learns from the reading and how it provides an escape from her personal struggles.*

What evidence is shown in this passage? The teacher:

- References the goal (expand Student A's reading repertoire).
- Gives specific examples of materials/strategies used to address the goal.
- Explains her actions (role) and the result (Student A can now find texts that interest her).
- Explains how the student has changed or grown in relation to the goal.

What Works

Give specific examples in your writing.

Why It Works

Each example is evidence that supports the effectiveness of your teaching.

WRITING TO MAKE THINKING VISIBLE IN THE STUDENT WORK ENTRY

Not explaining their thinking and decisions may be the most common error candidates make when writing the student work entry. It's easy to point out what the student(s) did or didn't do in a work sample, but too often candidates don't write about their own role within the learning sequence. Sometimes this is because the teacher's actions have become so automatic that the candidate doesn't consciously pay attention to them anymore. Other times the candidate simply fails to mention the choices and decisions made. This is a grave mistake in the National Board process. Although candidates write about student growth, what the National Board assessor is really looking for is evidence about the candidate's teaching practice. Don't let a blind spot undermine your writing when it comes to instructional decisions and choices *you make.*

What Works

- Write in the first person. Use "I" statements frequently.
- Use sentence starters or stems such as:

  I chose ___ because___.
  Because I know Tim ___, I ___.
  First I ___, then I followed up by ___.
  When I saw ___, I realized ___.
  The reasons I chose ___ were ___.
  I saw the error was caused by ___ so I ___.

As a result of ___ , Jennifer was able to ___ .
I used a variety of strategies including ___ , ___ , and ___ .

Why It Works

Explaining your actions makes your thinking visible. Using sentence stems that show cause and effect as evidence shows strong analysis.

The student work entry is really about examining your teaching practice through the lens of student work samples. Analyzing student work is among the most important things teachers do because it has such a significant impact on student learning. You are already experienced with this skill! But you may not have had to analyze and reflect on it in written form until now. Writing clearly, consistently, and convincingly showcases your accomplished teaching. This entry is an opportunity to let your expertise shine through.

CANDIDATE VIGNETTES

January: A Fresh Start?

Lynn

After the break, Lynn feels she's getting a fresh start. She's feeling healthier, and her energy is renewed. This time she's planning backwards for her Entry 2 video and finally gets one she feels will work. She takes the video and her Entry 4 draft to her cohort meeting for feedback and is relieved to be able to move on to Entry 1. She looks at the Focus Standards for Entry 1 and uses them to design lessons that will address the prompts. She plans to collect student work samples over the next two months. Having both videos is such a relief. She can continue to polish entries she's worked on and start writing Entry 2.

Rick

Over Winter Break, Rick studied the prompts for Entries 2 and 3 hoping to understand what he needs to show in each video. His CSP had suggested planning backwards starting with the video prompts. He films two lessons for Entry 3 and hopes there will be a useable segment. In one sequence, the camera operator presses the pause button by mistake and misses some good discussion, but the other segment shows promise. Other candidates have shown videos at previous meetings, and he decides he'll do that too, although he dreads having others watch. As his support group critiques his video, there are moments when Rick feels defensive and even angry. They have it so much easier than he does. However, he later watches the video again and sees the lack of evidence. Disappointed, he goes back to the drawing board for Entry 3.

Jan

Jan had the best intentions of choosing the segment of the video to feature in her writing during her Winter Break, but December was a bust. She had a project due for her reading endorsement and had to meet with her study group twice. Her younger son became ill, her church co-teacher was away, and her in-laws came for the holidays. Because she got so little done over the break, she signed up to attend a January weekend work session her cohort will host. The feedback she receives points out there is very little evidence of student-to-student interaction in her video because she talked too much and didn't give groups enough independence to have rich dialogue. Back to square one. However, she's learning from her setbacks. She decides to begin work on Entry 2 and start collecting student work samples for Entry 1. She has made up her mind that next month must be productive.

Chapter Eight

Writing the Video Entries: Entries 2 and 3

Six Word Memoir: I know. I do. I impact! —Paula, PA

STRESSED OUT

Let's be honest. For most candidates, making the videos creates the most frustration. Most certificates require two video entries, although the Music certificate requires three. Log onto any National Board Internet group or attend almost any candidate support meeting and you'll find teachers struggling to get a video that will "work." Horror stories about videotaping abound when any group of candidates or NBCTs gather. Getting a workable video segment is paramount because the bulk of a video entry can't be written until the segment is filmed and chosen. Most teachers tackle the video entries using these strategies:

- *Plan the Perfect Lesson.* In reality, there is no such thing as a perfect lesson, but candidates never stop trying to film one. It's logical to think that if the lesson is great, the video will be great too. But even a well-planned lesson can't always overcome the glitches that can occur: a disconnected cord, bad sound, a confrontational student, or the first time all year that your students had nothing to say.
- *Video Early and Video Often.* This makes sense. It can be helpful to film lessons for practice—to get yourself and your students comfortable with the camera. This strategy goes with the premise that if you film lots of lessons, eventually you'll get a segment that will work. This is the strategy I relied on. I taped 12 lessons for an entry before finally finding a segment for my small group video. By the end, my students and I were exhausted by the effort. It's one thing to film for practice and another to be clueless about filming. I estimate that it took close to 30 hours of viewing to find that magic 15 minute segment. If only I'd known then what I know now about the video entries, I'd have saved myself a lot of stress.

WHY VIDEO?

Start by understanding *why* the National Board asks you to do video entries.

- Video recorded teaching sessions offer particularly strong evidence of a candidate's pedagogical knowledge and ability to manage learning opportunities because the videos are snapshots of real lessons in real time.
- Videos allow the candidate to be in charge of what an assessor sees. The assessor sees only what you choose to submit. Did a student get sick? Don't use that part. Surprise fire drill while you are taping? Start over another time. You have the power and flexibility to determine what an assessor sees. Submitting videos is really a gift, an opportunity to show your real teaching practice on your terms.
- Videos are the best way to showcase the climate of a classroom, teaching and management strategies, student engagement, the discourse environment, and the interactions that take place during teaching and learning sequences. Assessors get a real glimpse of your classroom as well as the opportunity to view a snapshot of your teaching and your students' learning.
- It's hard to fake a productive learning environment if it doesn't really exist.

FILMING FRUSTRATIONS

Even though the rationale for video entries is powerful, getting one you want to use can be among the most frustrating aspects of the certification process. Why is that?

- Most of us hate seeing and hearing ourselves on video. We don't like our hair, our clothes, our weight, or our voices. We may discover vocal or physical mannerisms we weren't aware of. So a major obstacle is to get over ourselves. It takes some effort, but you can learn to concentrate on the content of the lesson instead of yourself. Consider it a major milestone when you conquer this hurdle.
- Technology and logistical issues can be frustrating and intimidating. Being unfamiliar with the equipment, arranging for someone to come in and film, figuring out how to film without any help, and poor sound quality all cause angst. Add in cords that come unplugged and challenging student behaviors, and you have the ingredients for a possible meltdown.

What Works: Video Smart!

The strategies of planning a perfect lesson and taping early and often aren't without merit. Everyone becomes accustomed to the camera and feels more comfortable. Along the way the logistical and technological challenges become more manageable.

But in truth, and this is what most candidates struggle with, the lesson you submit doesn't have to be perfect. Neither do the students or the teacher. In fact, a "perfect" video could give the appearance of being staged. The assessors aren't looking for a dog-and-pony show; they expect to see a real lesson. Dog-and-pony shows almost always backfire in some way. Real lessons give honest data to write about. The best way to "video smart" is to understand the prompts, learn what the assessors expect to see, plan a lesson that shows the standards you are asked to demonstrate, and keep the lesson real.

What Works: Designing the Lesson with the End in Mind—Plan Backward!

Like when planning the student work entry, an effective way to get a video that works is to plan *backwards*. Know your destination, and then plan the route to get there.

- Start with the prompts. Determine what the outcome of the prompt could look like.

- Brainstorm how to show the outcome in light of the goals and standards.
- Include as much of the evidence that assessors expect to see as possible.

Instead of blindly video-taping (except when just "practicing") and hoping the evidence is there, begin with the prompts and the evidence you need to demonstrate—then plan how to include that evidence. To illustrate the thinking that plays into this strategy, read prompts and hypothetical plans from *MCGEN* Entry 3 (Integrating Mathematics with Science), *EMC/LRLA* Entry 2 (Constructing Meaning through Reading), and *AYA/Science* Entry 2 (Active Scientific Inquiry). The planning process is the same for any certificate. I've written in first person to model the thinking process a candidate might use.

   MCGEN: *What evidence of inquiry, intellectual engagement, discussion, and content are demonstrated in your video recording? How did you further the students' knowledge and skills and engage them intellectually?*

- I'll show a discovery activity that the students find interesting so they will be highly engaged. *(inquiry and intellectual engagement)*
- I'll provide situations for students to talk with each other about the content, not just procedures or social talk. *(discussion and content)*
- I'll show I am moving them forward in their knowledge of the topic using more than just the textbook. *(inquiry and further students' knowledge of content)*
- I'll ask higher level questions, not ones that call for just a yes or no. *(intellectual engagement, further students' knowledge of content)*
- I'll choose a topic that is important in science and their daily lives. *(intellectual engagement and knowledge of content)*

EMC/LRLA: *How did you use teacher-to-student and, when appropriate, student-to-student interactions to further student(s) abilities to construct meaning? Cite an example from the video to describe how these interactions supported student(s) ability to construct meaning.*

- I'll have questions and prompts about the content and reading skills ready to ask. *(teacher-to-student interaction)*
- I'll engage each student in conversation about the content and/or skills. *(fosters construction of meaning/teacher-to-student interaction)*
- I'll set up opportunities for the students to talk with each other about the reading. *(student-to-student interaction)*

AYA/Science: *Citing specific evidence from the first segment of the video recording, how did you support student inquiry in order to conceptualize the primary questions and/or methodology of the investigation?*

- I need to plan and set up an investigation but not provide the entire rationale. *(supports student inquiry)*
- The investigation needs to be planned to foster *student* inquiry with variables and/or other valid methods of investigation. *(student inquiry, not teacher demonstration)*
- It can't be an investigation with totally predetermined steps where students simply read the directions and follow them in order to confirm expected results. *(learning science through inquiry and/or other appropriate methodology)*
- The investigation needs to be one that allows students to develop a rationale for the experimental processes they will use. *(promotes scientific thinking)*

Now that the hypothetical candidate has notes about what to plan as evidence for each prompt, the lesson can be structured following the *Architecture of Accomplished Teaching*. The candidate can be confident there will be evidence to write about for each prompt. In your real classroom, you may discover that your class needs up-front modeling and practice of the cooperative learning strategies, for example, and/or procedures you expect them to use for the activities *before* filming takes place. The day you film for real isn't the day to try something new.

WHAT ASSESSORS EXPECT TO SEE

This is what every candidate wants to know—what are the assessors looking for? It really isn't a secret; the clues are in the instructions. In every video, show these types of evidence:

* The goal or objective matches the instruction seen on the video.
* Multiple teaching strategies and options are evidenced.
* Teacher-to-student interaction occurs.
* Student-to-teacher interaction occurs.
* Student-to-student interaction occurs.
* Fairness, equity, access, and respect for diversity are evident.

What Works: Finding the Evidence Assessors Expect to See in an ECGen/MCGen Entry 3 Lesson

* *Goal Matches the Activity.* Goal: students learn about Newton's Laws of Motion (science). Activity: students roll small cars down ramps covered with various surfaces.
* *Multiple Strategies or Options.* Some students prepare ramps with various surfaces for an inquiry activity; others are engaged in snapping together Unifix cubes to use for measurement and gather cars to roll down the ramps; still others write their observations in their science journal. There is choice or differentiation of tasks, and information is presented in more than one way: perhaps in the forms of reading text, discussion, and a video.
* *Teacher-to-Student Interaction.* The teacher engages students in discourse or discussion about the motion of the cars as they roll down the ramp, asks open-ended questions, and asks them to compare, evaluate, explain, or defend an answer or approach.
* *Student to Teacher Interaction.* A student question or comment may spark a back and forth exchange. The teacher has comments or questions ready to encourage responses and notes misconceptions or interactions that occur that indicate understanding.
* *Student-to-Student Interaction.* The teacher listens for misconceptions or understandings expressed as students work together. Each member of the group is responsible for part of the inquiry activity.
* *Inquiry and Math Integration.* Students test a variable during their investigation and integrate math in a meaningful way. They measure distance and/or time.
* *Fairness, Equity, and Access for All Students and Respect for Diversity.* The teacher demonstrates that each student's uniqueness is valued by describing how the differentiated goals, instruction, and assessments meet students' needs. Examples include:

  * Providing preferential seating and appropriate assistance.
  * Recognizing learning styles, cultural values, and examples of fair play.
  * Giving each student the opportunity to do both activities.

- Explaining why students are grouped in a certain way; explaining why the student in the blue shirt uses a spelling device when writing or why only student A was allowed to use a particular tool or technology.

Why It Works

Making those elements evident in the video provides strong support and evidence and lends validity to the Written Commentary.

The video shows the *what*, the writing explains the *why*. It's a reasonable assumption that if the lesson is well planned—for both content and the evidence assessors expect to see—you stand a better chance of creating a segment that works without exhausting yourself and your students by filming over and over. You still may need several attempts, but you increase the odds that you won't be trying to get a usable video segment at the last minute or in a panic.

Because the standards are embedded within the evidence, the video segments that include as much evidence as possible may be ones that will work. The purpose of the video is to *support* the Written Commentary, so the assessors first read the entry, then watch the video, and finally read the entry again to verify the meshing of the two.

DEMONSTRATING THE STANDARDS

The Standards contain multiple examples to help you plan and recognize evidence in your own practice. At the beginning of each entry is a list of Standards that are significant to that entry. At each planning step, ask what could occur in the video to show that Standard. For example, when students are engaged in a discussion that deepens their understanding, what Standard is evident? When students interact with each other, what Standard is evident? When students are able to make choices, what Standard is evident? Often something in a video will evidence more than one Standard. Appendix Figure 8.1 can help you find and list the evidence in your video.

LOOKING FOR CLUES IN THE INSTRUCTIONS AND RUBRIC

Reading the portfolio instructions thoroughly is the only way to identify evidence that assessors expect to see. It's also important to be familiar with the Level 4 rubric, which explains the 3 Cs: *clear, consistent, convincing* evidence. Many specific examples of evidence are included in the explanation of each standard, and incorporating these makes a stronger case for your accomplished teaching. Reading the standards and highlighting specific strategies that are appropriate for your students, at this time, in this setting will move you in the right direction. All of these contain clues about the types of evidence key to each entry. For example:

- If a prompt asks for *specific evidence of students' understanding, misunderstandings, misconceptions, errors and/or progress shown on the video,* be sure to include several examples in your writing. There may not be examples of all of those items.
- General responses are usually not strong evidence. Be specific.
- Use the key words in the prompt to point to specific examples from the video.

Example from AYA/Math: *Group 1 used the decimal approximation of 0.333 for the scale factor instead of using 1/3. As a result, their equation produced outputs that almost matched the data. This was an unintended opportunity to discuss the appropriateness of rounding when creating equations, and while it was not one of the intended learning goals, the small group format allowed me to explore this concept with the group.*

WHAT DOES EVIDENCE LOOK LIKE?

Here are some places to look and listen for evidence or examples in a video. Pay attention to:

- What is said.
- What is done.
- What questions are asked.
- Facial expressions.
- Body language.
- Level of engagement.
- Interactions.
- Instructional materials.
- Goals and objectives (Big Idea of Science).
- Strategies.
- Assessments.

Each of the above is connected to one or more of the Five Core Propositions and hence to one or more Standards. If assessors see the above evidence in your video, and if you write about the evidence with specific examples, you will produce a strong entry.

What Works: Being Specific!

Citing *specific examples* of the above evidence is the best way to provide the clear, consistent, and convincing evidence called for in the Level 4 rubric. The key word is *specific!* Following are some *hypothetical* examples:

- Because I knew that Todd struggled to find the area of a quadrilateral, I gave him a set of centimeter cubes to practice filling the interior spaces of square and rectangle shapes. At the beginning of the video, he uses the cubes to fill the shapes (find the area). Next he draws his own squares on graph paper. At the end of the video, he explains the process to his partner. This showed me that he was catching onto the concept of *area* so he could soon apply the formula to quadrilaterals.
- The girl in the red sweater repeatedly insisted that insects had eight legs, so I matched her with a compatible partner to read *The Wonderful World of Insects* together. Later in the video, she correctly drew an insect that has six legs.
- Group 1 made several unsuccessful attempts to assemble the model. They were arguing, so I approached them and asked what procedure they had followed so far. I asked the group to come up with a strategy that would help them assemble the model without missing any steps. Their solution was to ask Group 3 to show them the steps they had used to complete the model. While watching Group 3, Richard realized that they had not matched the parts correctly and pointed this out to his partners. After that, Group 1 was able to return to their model and complete it successfully.

Why It Works

Specific examples are where evidence is found.

What Works: Choosing the Video Segment

- Read the instructions so you are crystal clear about the requirements regarding time, grouping, number of segments, editing, and panning the room, for example. Directions must be followed exactly. They are the final word.
- Know the *maximum* number of minutes specified in the instructions.
- A segment can be *shorter* than the maximum number of minutes allowed.
- Follow the *20 Percent Rule*: a video should not be more than 20 percent shorter than the maximum minutes allowed. Thus, a video with a 15 minute maximum should probably not be shorter than about 12 minutes.

Watch the entire lesson once to get a sense of its quality. Then, once you have some promising footage, use Appendix Figure 8.2 to analyze and record the evidence you find. Try these strategies to locate a usable segment.

What Works: Watching the Segment Multiple Times

- *Watch the first time* to verify the goal and objectives are evident and that they match.
- *Watch the second time* with the sound off to watch for body language and facial expressions that indicate student engagement and interactions.
- *Watch the third time* with only sound (turn your back to the screen). Listen for exchanges between the teacher and students, between students and teacher, and among students, as well as discourse about the content.
- *Watch the fourth time* with your class. The comments they make can be insightful! It's guaranteed that they will notice things you didn't, and you can include these in the analysis and reflection sections.
- Watching the video with colleagues and other candidates is also an effective strategy.

What Works: Documenting the Standards in the Video

Review the video segment for evidence of the Standards listed in each entry and in the Level 4 rubric. Note the evidence you find.

- What did you do and say?
- What did the students do and say?
- What interactions took place between people?
- What interactions took place with the content?
- What did you do to promote a climate of learning?
- Are all of the components and sections in the entry instructions addressed?
- Did you respond to *all parts* of the prompt and questions?
- Consider eliminating parts showing directions or transitions because this section may lack evidence.

Let's return to the sample scenario described earlier to analyze which standards might be demonstrated by the student to student interaction described. The scenario: *Part of the class participates in an inquiry activity with ramps while the others write in their science journal. Each member is responsible for helping to determine the surface of his or her ramp. They have all received direct instruction and completed other activities to build foundational knowledge about force and motion. All will have opportunity to complete both activities.*

Continuing with the MCGen Certificate Standards, here are possible ways the Standards could be evidenced. Note the use of the first person to model the writing style. Using the first person ensures that the teacher is visible within the lesson.

Writing about Knowledge of Students

- *I arranged* groups to address student strengths and needs and assigned jobs within the group to address learning strengths, needs, interests, and language fluency.
- *I presented* instruction, materials, and activities that are age appropriate. They show my knowledge and understanding of how to organize and manage learning.

Writing about Knowledge of Content and Curriculum

- *I addressed* a Big Idea of Science and planned appropriate goals and objectives.
- *I taught* information that was accurate and connected to real life.
- *I integrated* the topic with other subject areas (including math required for the entry) and used appropriate technology to support it.

Writing about Instructional Decision Making

- *I planned* a discovery (inquiry) activity and product that fostered inquiry and required students to explain their thinking.
- *I provided* a variety of nonfiction materials to foster reading skills and extend and enrich learning.
- *I asked* students to demonstrate ways the topic applies to real life.
- *I gave* students choices in how they showed their knowledge of the water cycle.
- *I presented* the core knowledge in a variety of ways.
- *I planned* activities to address various learning styles and students' strengths.
- *I used* a variety of assessments to determine student progress.
- *Students showed* their knowledge in various ways including writing science journals and making presentations.
- *I evaluated* the success of the unit and planned for the next steps.

Writing about Reflective Practice

- *I analyzed* the results of the assessments in order to know whether instruction was successful and decide where to go next.
- *I realized* I needed to re-teach the concept of condensation because students had not yet corrected misconceptions.

The above points are examples of how to address and write about the standards your entry emphasizes in the Analysis of the Video Recording section of the entry. Note as well how the standards connect to the Architecture of Accomplished Teaching.

FINALIZING THE DETAILS

- *Select* a segment that demonstrates the *most* evidentiary support and is richest with the Standards and Level 4 rubric evidence.

- *Find* a segment that fits the time-frame in the instructions.
- *Use* a stop-watch or the time print for exact times.
- *List* the standards evidenced.
- *List* the specific examples you can use as evidence.
- *Upload* the chosen segment onto your National Board Portal for submission.
- *Follow* formatting and labeling directions exactly!
- *Call* 1-800-22TEACH with questions. Rely only on your instructions and/or the NBPTS for information!

What Works: Filming the Lesson

The information contained in your NBPTS Portfolio Directions Part I regarding filming techniques is comprehensive and the definitive word. But here is a list of additional tips.

- Have release forms signed and kept in a safe place for all students and adults being filmed. Those without permission can be seated out of camera range.
- Film using a digital camera or other device such as an iPad or even an iPhone or smartphone.
- Be sure you can upload your format onto your e-submission portal.
- Learn to ignore the camera, and teach your students to do the same. If using a digital camera, set the camera up often, but put tape over the "on" light so that it becomes just another object in the room.
- Consider having a student operate the camera if using a tripod.
- Set the tripod at student eye level, which may mean placing the camera or device on a low table or even the floor.
- Have sturdy extension cords available, and use them safely (taped to the floor).
- Use an external microphone with groups if possible. This isn't possible with all devices.
- Show the faces of the students and teacher.
- The teacher's face should clearly show at least every 5 minutes. The camera should focus mainly on students to showcase their discussion and actions.
- Don't make the video all "teacher talk."
- Don't "stage" any lesson. Forget the dog-and-pony show. "Real" is honest, natural, and gives you real material to write about. "Fake" is unethical and almost always backfires.
- Turn off fans, aquarium pumps, and so forth when possible to avoid extraneous noise.
- Pan the room s-l-o-w-l-y if your directions say to do so.
- Pay attention to what you wear. The assessors receive bias training, but you still want to appear professional. Think about what might be hanging out, hanging over, or show when you bend over.
- Allow yourself one "pity-party" to moan and groan about your hair, your voice, your weight, or whatever other faults you perceive you have. Then get over yourself so you can focus on the content of the video!
- *The biggest video mistakes*: The teacher talks too much; not enough student to student talk; too much procedural talk; not enough content talk.

MORE FILMING TIPS

- Read your directions very carefully so that you know exactly what grouping a particular entry asks for. The instructions are the final word!

- If you have no camera operator: place the camera or device on a tripod near the front, off to one side, to film a whole group. You can move the camera whenever needed. You don't need to be visible every minute, but your face should show at least every 5 minutes.
- Carry the camera or device to a location, set it down to capture a group, and walk in and out of the frame if needed. Turn the camera around occasionally to show your face.
- The camera or device can be on a tripod focused on one location, a table for example, and groups can move to and from the table. It's ok to show short transitions.
- Have the camera operator follow you from group to group, but it's permissible for them to also pan the room occasionally or focus on one group for an interval.
- Do everything possible to have student voices heard. It helps the assessors and saves you from needing to do extensive transcription in the writing.

The video is support for your written commentary and doesn't need to be perfect. Plan some logistics for filming, but keep them as simple as possible.

WRITING THE VIDEO ENTRY: DESCRIBE, ANALYZE, AND REFLECT

Every entry requires three types of writing: description, analysis, and reflection, and each prompt can call for one or more of the three types of writing. The borders between the types can be fuzzy, but keep the following generalities in mind:

- *Description* is an objective retelling to give the reader a sense of being in the classroom. It answers the questions *what* and *which*. Key verbs are *describe, state, list,* and *define*.
- *Analysis* reveals the thought processes used to make instructional decisions and explains the significance and impact of evidence submitted. Analysis involves the interpretation of the facts. Key analysis questions are *why, how,* and *so what*. Key words are *analyze, explain, because, in order to,* and *interpret*.
- *Reflection* deals with the thought processes that occur after a teaching situation. It is hindsight and takes place in order to improve future teaching practices. The key reflection question is *now what?* Reflection cues include *improve, change,* and *in the future*.

VOCABULARY IN THE VIDEO PROMPTS

- The Climate in the Classroom. How factors such as the nature of the learning experience, the degree of intellectual risk-taking encouraged by the teacher, respect, fairness, equity, access, and classroom management come together.
- Student Engagement with the Content. The extent to which the students are actively involved in the learning
- Interactions. Verbal and non-verbal interaction between the teacher and students, between the students and the teacher, and among the students.
- Discourse Environment. The nature of the discussion which occurs, the role of the teacher in promoting inquiry and debate, and the student responses.

What Works: Writing about Evidence in the Video

- The video itself isn't scored, but it's evidence to support the Written Commentary.
- Point out your teaching behaviors. Some, such as questioning strategies, are obvious, while others, like using an attention signal or body language, are more subtle.

- Refer to specific moments and explain what you were thinking when you said a particular thing or took a particular action. Even if an action is obvious, explaining the rationale behind it will make the writing more convincing.
- Describe any adjustments you made during the lesson and tell why.
- Point out any "aha" moments that occur in student understanding.
- You can refer to students using an identifying characteristic, such as *the blond boy,* or by first name.
- You can use a time reference if you have space and feel it will help the assessors find the evidence: *At 7:54 I addressed Tony's misconception that all heavy objects sink.*
- If it is difficult to hear something important, you can script the dialogue: *When the volcano erupted, the boy in the red shirt said, "The liquid spurting out is magma."* However, try not to do this too often because it consumes valuable space.
- Call attention to student engagement. Remember to include the more subtle signs such as eye contact, body language, posture, and taking notes. Engagement doesn't always have to be active movement or talk.
- If a student's behavior is problematic, don't discard a video for that reason alone. It may allow you to discuss challenges you deal with (possibly also mentioned in the Instructional Context), and your rationale for addressing the behavior.
- Use *specific examples* from the video: *Mike was able to borrow successfully when he subtracted.* Make this your mantra!
- State and explain your rationales for decisions you make and actions you take.

Why It Works

Presenting evidence in the video entries is not about looking a particular way, sounding a particular way, or teaching a particular way. The video is not meant to be a Hollywood production. It is about showing your teaching practice in an honest way—giving a snapshot of what you really do and how you really teach. It's about how you plan, how you respond, and how you impact student learning using your own teaching style, your understanding of your students, and your pedagogical knowledge. You must specifically point this evidence out in your writing.

Fabricated Writing Examples

AYA/Math

At 12:45, Group 5 uses both calculators and their smartphones to calculate the growth or decay factors and find initial values of the exponential equation they created. Justin shares his findings with his group, but others got a different answer. Logan then leans over Justin's desk and goes over the steps again. This time Justin's results are correct.

WLOE/French

Each group had a scenario about traveling, and they were to use vocabulary and grammatical structures to check in at a hotel, arrive at the airport, or plan a sight-seeing trip. At 2:21, Group 1 works together to give directions in French to a hotel from the airport. Monique, in blue, creates a map using directional words and place names. She struggles with the pronunciation of the place names, and others in her group can be heard correcting her. However, the group members also were not saying the place names correctly, so I went to the group and had them echo my pronunciation. As a result, all their pronunciation improved.

EA/ELA

I used a two-circle Socratic circle as the format for this lesson. To help students participate who were struggling, I encouraged them to look back at their notes from the previous class, so they could find information and be able to participate in the discussion. I do this at 5:16 in the video when the blonde boy in the green shirt was not prepared to speak. I asked him to look back at what he wrote on Friday. As a result he was able to participate in the discussion.

EMC/LRLA

I incorporated differentiation into the graphic organizers by providing varying degrees of information on organizers. At 4:29, Louis, in black, works on a cloze sentence graphic organizer because he needs more teacher assistance. Marie had sentence starters to foster more independent work, while Liz, who works above grade level, had space for taking notes. They talk together about the Thomas Edison video they watched and the cause and effect of his experiments. Stewart asks Marie why Edison had so many failures, and Marie replies "Because he had to try a lot of different ideas to see what worked and what didn't," which shows understanding of cause and effect on Marie's part and helped clarify the concept for Stewart.

ECGen

For the most part the students raised their hands and waited their turns, which is evidence of the social skill for this lesson. At 6:12 and 6:27 I redirected some the students' attention. There are some occasions when one student talks over another one, like at 6:38 when the girl in the red shirt is talking about Rapunzel; but no one gets upset or verbalizes that it is "their turn."

EAYA/PE

At 42:12, Dan asked what would happen if two people tagged each other simultaneously during the game. This was significant because Dan is often seen as the underdog by his peers. After the game, at 47:00, I complimented him for asking that question. I probed, asking him how his peers' reactions made him feel during the game today. He stated, "Good because I think it helped everyone play fair because I asked a question that could solve a problem before it happened."

Note the use of the first person and active-voice verbs: *I knew, I went, I encouraged, I asked, I do, I incorporated, I redirect, I showed, I probed.* This makes the teacher's intentions clear, keeps the teacher's thinking and actions visible, and uses less space.

CANDIDATE VIGNETTES

February: So Much to Do

Lynn

Lynn's school is vandalized one weekend, and her classroom is trashed. The computers in her classroom are damaged, and paperwork is scattered everywhere. The vandals splattered paint all around the room, including on some of the student work she saved for Entry 1. She's working on Entries 2 and 3 on her computer at home, but Entry 4 was on her classroom computer; she lost all of her Entry 4 work. Thankfully, she has all her notes and can start over, but she's feeling the time pressure. This has been a blatant reminder to back up all computer work. Her goal is to be ready to submit on April 1, the first day the NBPTS will accept submissions, and this has disrupted her time line. After sorting through the undamaged student work samples, she salvages samples from two students and begins work on Entry 1. She starts rewriting Entry 4 as well.

Rick

Rick is feeling pressure to move forward. He is about half finished with Entry 4 and has started writing Entry 1 but isn't finished with any entry yet. He still needs both videos. Who knew this would be so hard? In the past he'd been able to knock out papers and projects quickly and with ease. Sometimes he feels frustrated about the things the National Board asks candidates to show, but Rick redoubles his efforts to get videos for Entries 2 and 3. He films several lessons, trying to take into account the issues that had kept the previous videos from working. This time, before filming, he researches some cooperative learning and discussion strategies and teaches them to his class. He makes an effort to talk less so the kids can talk with each other more. He looks at the prompts in the Video Analysis section of each entry and plans topics and activities that let his students demonstrate evidence of them. Amazingly, once he does those things, things fall into place and he gets two useable videos.

Jan

Finally, this month Jan gets a video for Entry 3, which means she can begin writing the Planning and Instruction and Video Analysis sections of the Written Commentary. Until now she's had nothing to share at her cohort meetings. It's still hard to find time to write because of all her other commitments. She'll finish the Reading Endorsement this month, which will free up some time, but she also needs some additional weekend time. She makes a pact with her husband to take the kids out for a few hours each weekend so she can have some uninterrupted blocks of time. She also convinces her church co-teacher to take over the class through May. Both these steps help create work time for Jan. She makes several videos for Entry 2, and things go much smoother. On the third attempt, she gets a workable video.

Chapter Nine

Writing about Documented Accomplishments: Entry 4

Six Word Memoir: How does this impact student learning? —Danielle, PA

WHAT IS A DOCUMENTED ACCOMPLISHMENT?

A documented accomplishment is an activity that is an added dimension of your work. Accomplishments are activities or events that go above and beyond a teacher's routine job expectations and impact student learning. What have you done beyond the textbook or science kit, after hours, and on your own that exemplifies accomplished teaching as described in your NBPTS Standards? Entry 4 asks teachers to provide evidence of professional activities that show them as learners, leaders and collaborators with colleagues, and partners with families and the community.

The following may help you understand those categories better:

- Learner. *Within the past five years,* you have engaged in ongoing professional development beyond that required by your district that impacted student learning and strengthened your knowledge and skills relevant to your teaching practice.
- Leader/Collaborator. *Within the past five years,* you have worked with colleagues to share your expertise in a collaborative and/or leadership role to improve teaching and/or student learning within the school or wider professional community.
- Partner with Families. *In the current year,* show how you involve parents and other interested adults in your students' education; how you promote ongoing, mutually beneficial interactions between students and the wider community; and how you foster *two-way* dialogue with parents and other interested adults (special area teachers, social workers, school psychologist, etc.) These must also show an *impact on student learning*.

Note: There are also ways to show your partnership with families *over the past five years*. For example, if you have hosted a yearly family event or have consistently trained parent volunteers *and* these events are ongoing and can be tied to impact on student learning, you could consider them. However, there must also be evidence for the *current year*.

When starting the National Board Certification process, many candidates gravitate toward Entry 4 because it doesn't require a video or student work samples. It's the only entry that can be started during the summer or early in the school year before instruction is in full gear. And it's the only entry not organized around the Architecture of Accomplished Teaching. At first glance it may seem easier than other entries; after all, there are only three questions to answer about each accomplishment. But it is more complex that it appears on the surface—like peeling layers away from an onion.

IT'S ABOUT YOUR IMPACT ON STUDENT LEARNING

On the surface, it sounds like this entry is all about you—the wonderful things you've done, the awards you've won, and the accolades you've received. And it is—partly. But when you dig deeper, you'll see that it's actually about showing what *impact on student learning* your development as a learner, leader and collaborator, and partner with families and your community has had. Providing evidence that an accomplishment impacted student learning is what it's all about.

WHY CANDIDATES BOMB THIS ENTRY

If Entry 4 seems easiest, why do many candidates get their lowest score on this entry? The main reason is a *lack of evidence of impact on student learning*. It's a misconception that candidates who score low didn't have accomplishments "worthy" enough. The real issue isn't the worthiness of the accomplishments; it's that the candidate failed to connect them to student learning. The point missed is that many ordinary-sounding activities can have strong connections to student learning while some razzle-dazzle ones don't. The bottom line is that *each accomplishment must show impact on student learning*. That can't be over-stressed.

What Works: Choose Smart, Choose Strong

- *Less May Be More in Entry 4.* Use only your strongest accomplishments that are unequiv-ocally connected to student learning. Although eight is the maximum number of accom-plishments allowed, there is no magic number that assures a bankable score. Consider having between three and six accomplishments to show you are well-rounded but allows space to write in-depth. The challenge is to sift through what may be a long list of ideas to find ones most strongly connected to impact on student learning. Avoid overkill! It's quality, not quantity that counts.
- *Show Yourself as a Learner, Leader/Collaborator, and Family/Community Partner.*

    Learner. Use trainings, classes, workshops, endorsements, and conferences.
    Leader. Leading workshops; chairing committees; initiating an action that brought something new to your school, district, or grade level; or organizing a parent or community event are possible accomplishments.
    Collaborator. Serving on committees, grade level teams, or school improvement panels or working with families are possibilities if they connect to student learning.
    Family/Community Partner. Show *two-way* communication with families *during the current school year*. This is crucial even for middle school and high school teachers. You must clearly show that you have *ongoing, back-and-forth communication* with students' families.
    Use Appendix Figure 9.1 to brainstorm and categorize your potential accomplishments.

- *Establish Two-way Communication.* Having a website or writing a newsletter is worthwhile, but unless it is interactive and includes a way for parents to respond and provide feedback, the communication doesn't flow in two directions. Interactive, two-way communication methods such weekly folders, notes, and surveys can work. If some of your methods move information in only one direction, consider adding a way others can respond such as a tear-off section on a newsletter or an email link on your website.
- *Keep a Communication Log.* Candidates want to know if keeping a Communication Log is required. On page 2-45 of Entry 4, the National Board states that submitting a Communication Log is not mandatory, but "we encourage you to submit a sampling of a page if you use one." The fact that the instructions imply such encouragement shows that the National Board clearly values the information a log provides. This is obvious from the amount of space they devote to it. In their eyes, it shows you've gone "above and beyond" routine efforts to build communication. It's a way to document contacts that don't lend themselves to other forms of documentation such as artifacts or verification forms.

A Communication Log sample and blank template are included in your National Board materials for this purpose, and according to the Level 4 scoring rubric, the two-way communication should be primarily focused on academics (substantive teaching and learning issues). So, for example, a phone log that documents a mix of communications about academic and behavioral issues may be stronger than one that covers behavior problems only. Appendix Figure 9.2 is a modified Communication Log template created for your use.

A comprehensive two-way communication process might look like something this:

- Through your communication with a parent, you learn something new or important about a student. Using that knowledge, you change an aspect of your teaching practice that impacts the student's learning and share that growth with the parent.
- *Or* the parent takes an action with their child that you have suggested.
- *Or* a special area teacher contacts you about an issue with one of your students. This initiates conversation that leads to a solution to the problem.

This process shows an assessor that a teacher isn't just closing the classroom door and doing his or her own thing without input from others. Teachers who seek *two-way* communication from those who know their students best and use what has been shared to improve their teaching practice show that they value the input and are responsive to parental concerns.

- *Address Multiple Areas.* Many accomplishments evidence more than one category. If you attend a math conference and learn new material that you teach your own students, and then plan a workshop to share the material, you show yourself as a learner and a leader/collaborator. If your grade level decides to plan a parent night to share strategies to use at home with their student, that shows learning, collaboration, leadership, and parent involvement.
- *Impact on Student Learning Can Be Direct or Indirect.* Direct impact involves your own students. Indirect impact occurs when student learning takes place as a result of someone else's interaction with you, such as when a colleague uses the ideas gained at the workshop *you* led with her own students and it impacts their learning.

What Works: Showcasing Your Accomplishments

- *Use a Single Activity or Event as an Accomplishment.* Be comprehensive and explain the significance on your teaching and the impact on student learning extensively and in detail.

- *Group the Accomplishments.* If you have multiple accomplishments in a particular area, you can group them together under one title. Example: if you have several activities grouped around technology, you can write them as one accomplishment.
- *Title Your Accomplishments.* Instead of just naming the committee, activity, or event, give the accomplishment a title that points the assessor toward the evidence that showcases what you did and your role. Examples: *Math/Science/Language Arts Coordinator; Community Partnerships; Team Collaboration; Parent Partnerships; Colonial Days Fair Coordinator; Assessment Coordinator; Math/Science Liaison.* This works particularly well when an accomplishment addresses more than one category.
- *What Not to Choose.* Sometimes it's hard to explain why certain activities, especially ones teachers do with passion, aren't the best choices for Entry 4. Sponsorship of clubs or winning awards seldom work because they can be difficult to tie into academic student learning. And sometimes they don't address the categories you are asked to document. Even an accomplishment as valuable as a master's degree, while showing you as a learner, is so broad that documenting its impact on student learning is difficult.

Committees can also present challenges. They show collaboration but are often directed toward the "business" or "structure" of education and deal with adult issues rather than student learning. Analyze the purpose of committees you serve on or groups you sponsor to be sure they have an impact on student learning before choosing one to use. Appendix Figure 9.3 shows examples of how you might combine activities into one accomplishment.

Accomplishment Examples: Consider activities you've done in these areas *if* they can be tied to student learning:

- Creative or innovative use of technology
- Student advocacy
- Contributing to solving problems in your school or district
- Serve as a mentor to new or struggling teachers or with student teachers
- Community outreach that resulted in student success in a your subject area
- Leadership roles
- Designing or coordinating curriculum or other learning opportunities
- Sponsoring or participating in an activity that involves students and learning
- Promoting your subject area
- Presenting or coordinating staff development
- Cross-curricular collaboration with colleagues
- Bringing in community resources
- Enlisting parents to take an active role in their children's education

Why It Works

Choosing accomplishments with strong ties to academic learning affords your best opportunities to show evidence of impact on student learning.

What Works: Documenting Smart and Documenting Strong

- *Document Your Accomplishments in the Strongest Ways You Can.* The documentation you choose must not only verify that you did what you say you did but also support your claim of impact on student learning. Documentation that shows student growth *as a result of your efforts* is ideal if possible.

- *Verification Forms Are Considered Equal with Any Other Type of Verification.* Use these when your accomplishment doesn't leave a paper trail. They may be completed by anyone who can comment on your description of the activity, its accuracy, and its impact.
- *Document Every Accomplishment.* Choose the strongest evidence you can find that highlights the impact on student learning. Examples of documentation that show evidence of student learning include but are not limited to:

  Letters. From teachers, parents, students

  Emails. From parents, teachers, and colleagues

  Feedback Forms and Surveys. From colleagues at workshops you led, parents who attended a parent night event, or students after a unit of study, activity, or event

  Data. If available from before and after implementation to show growth as a result of your accomplishment.

Appendix Figure 9.4 shows one way to ask a colleague or parent for documentation of an accomplishment. *Note:* A piece of documentation can be used for only *one* accomplishment.

What Works: Writing Smart and Writing Strong

The following are suggestions based on feedback from assessors, writing coaches, candidates who certified, and personal experience. You won't find them in your National Board materials, but they are valid strategies for this type of academic writing.

- *Use the Candy Corn Analogy for Documented Accomplishments.* Don't laugh! It's not as silly as it may sound! You may have seen an illustration for this entry that shows a triangle divided into three horizontal sections—one for each question you'll answer per accomplishment. Visualize the triangle as a piece of candy corn. The tiny white tip at the top represents the nature of the accomplishment, the middle-sized yellow center shows the accomplishment's significance, and the deep, wide orange band at the bottom represents the impact on student learning. The visual in Appendix Figure 9.5 works well for Entry 4.
- *Follow the 10 Percent Rule in the "Nature of" Section.* This *must* be the shortest section because it is the least important and least evidentiary. It's the *so what?* section. You tell what you did, but keep it short and to the point. There is virtually no evidence is in this section, and only evidence earns points.
- *Follow the 40 Percent Rule in the Significance Section.* The significance is about *you, your actions,* and *why and how it impacted* you *as a teacher.* This is the *so what?* section—why it matters. Here you lay out your case with *reasons why* an accomplishment was important—*why* it matters to you, your teaching context, your grade level, your school, or your district.

  You may have perceived a need and then took an action to address it—either within your own teaching practice or beyond it. Here you lay the groundwork for evidence that is a *result of* the action you took and which led to the *impact* on student learning. Be specific. Something might be significant because it added to your knowledge base, you learned new strategies, it brought a new program to your school, other teachers learned and implemented a new skill or program because of your actions, or it changed your practice in some way. There can be a lot of evidence in the significance section. Appendix Figure 9.6 outlines examples and criteria for determining the significance of your accomplishments.
- *Follow the 50 Percent Rule in the Impact Section.* Impact is about the *kids*. Here you relate specifics and details about the activity. This is another *so what?* section, but it documents

the *impact on student learning* and is where most of your evidence is shown. This should be the longest and most detailed section for each accomplishment.

The more specific you can be with examples, the stronger the evidence. Consider using student examples, small group or whole group achievements, or impact on a grade level, school, or district. Avoid ambiguous phrases such as "I feel that . . . ," "It was fun . . . ," or "He began liking math more." Instead use specifics such as assessment results, documentation that shows an increase in the frequency that homework is turned in, or a decrease in the number of behavior referrals which meant that a student spent more time in class.

- Note: *The 10–40–50 Percent Rule Is* Not *a National Board Rule.* It's an amalgamation of advice and experience from assessors and NBCTs. One size may not fit all. There is wiggle room in the percentages. The point is to give parameters to keep the description shortest and the significance and impact sections longer because they contain most of the evidence that the assessors are looking for.

Showing Impact: Where ever you can, show impact on student learning through examples that use positive language:

- Juan's scores improved by an average of 15 points since . . .
- Sean's class ranking rose from near the bottom to the top half after . . .
- Laura is now checking out books three levels higher than when she entered the program.
- Madison's mother called to share how much she appreciates . . .
- For the first time this year, Sophie completed . . . because . . .

Why It Works

Writing more and writing positively in the significance and impact sections provides better evidence. Description contains little or no evidence.

What Works: Writing Strategies Recap

In cooking, the proof is in the pudding. But in National Board entries the proof is in the writing. Assessors are trained to find evidence anywhere it occurs, but clear writing can help them find it more easily. Here is a quick reminder of effective strategies for this entry:

- Write "I" statements using first-person pronouns like *I, my, mine,* and *myself.*
- Use strong, active verbs and phrases to describe what you have done. Purge your writing of as many verbs with helpers and *–ing* verb forms as possible. Active verb examples: *I/my students designed, implemented, organized, learned, measured, planned, provided, taught, analyzed, documented, supplied, questioned, grew, developed, engaged, collaborated, presented, attended, tried, wrote, let, read, sought, studied, visited, took, enhanced, modeled, improved, helped, invited, reflected, prepared, researched, encouraged, integrated, adopted, challenged, featured, realized, pointed out.*
- Use "we" sparingly. If explaining collaboration, use it once, then return to "I" statements.
- Avoid "touchy-feely" verbs and phrases such as *I feel . . . , I was proud . . . ,* and *I was honored . . .*
- Use adverbs to your advantage. Words like *effectively, appropriately, skillfully, positively, fully,* and many others provide powerful language.
- Control your style, tone, and persona. You don't want to be whiny, preachy, or rigid.
- Use a gender neutral style where possible.

- Avoid negative or judgmental observations or tone.
- Use language that portrays you as a student-centered teacher focused on student success.

Why It Works

The Level 4 rubric criteria requires evidence that it is clear, consistent, and convincing, and these strategies can help you make wise writing choices.

What Works: Writing the Reflection Summary

This two-page section is very important; don't skimp on it! It must truly be reflective and not just rehash or summarize what you've written before. It may be as important as all of your accomplishments put together! Reflection is a kind of self-analysis. It looks backward and forward and implies that you have thought about your accomplishments and developed some insights. It explains what you've learned from your experiences and looks for patterns or themes within your teaching practice. Reflection also includes plans for the future based on what you've done in the past. This is your opportunity to address and remedy any issues you encountered. It requires you to "fish in deeper waters" and thoughtfully examine where you are professionally and where you might go next. Assessors look at this part very carefully because it reveals what you have learned about yourself as a teacher. They are looking for evidence of personal growth, self-examination, and introspection.

What Works: Thinking and Writing about Your Thinking in the Reflection

- Identify patterns and themes in your practice.
- Determine which roles (learner, leader/collaborator, partner) seem to predominate in your accomplishments. For example, in my own entry, I found the pattern of teacher-leader and used that as the basis for reflection.
- Write about any personal insights you've gained through this process.
- What plan do you have for addressing any shortcomings?
- What have you learned from what you "see" when you examine your practice?
- If you worked on this entry early in your candidacy, return to it and reflect again. Your understanding of your teaching practice will have deepened considerably over time.

Why It Works

Many teachers score lowest on Entry 4 because they don't clearly explain the significance, don't connect the accomplishments to the impact on student learning, or don't truly and thoroughly reflect. Those elements are absolutely essential and must be the deciding factors when choosing accomplishments to include and when writing the Reflective Summary.

CANDIDATE VIGNETTES

March: Breakthroughs

Lynn

Finally Lynn has a month with no disasters. Her committee and department responsibilities are still time consuming, but she's able to move forward with every entry. The Written Commentary for Entry 1 is more difficult than she had imagined. She has to analyze the student work more deeply than she ever has before to address the prompts. In the past she has put minimal effort into writing assignments, but after completing Entry 1, she sees deeper value in them and vows to do them more often. Spring Break comes at the end of March, and Lynn spends most of the break editing and polishing her four entries. She also sorts through and chooses the documentation and verifications she's collected for Entry 4.

Rick

Getting the videos was a major coup because Rick can start writing in earnest. He now wishes he'd taken his CSP's advice and started writing earlier. Rick spends hours over Spring Break watching videos and choosing the segments. He finds that he needs to do some scripting of the videos because sometimes it's hard to hear what students say. This is time consuming but provides some important specific evidence to use. By the end of Spring Break, Rick has roughed out drafts for Entries 2 and 3, which feels good. Now he has to finish Entries 1 and 4.

Jan

At last, Jan feels she's making steady progress. She has two videos and a fair amount of writing on Entries 2 and 3. She is still collecting work samples for Entry 1. She realizes she hasn't worked on Entry 4 in a long time, so she revisits it and makes a number of revisions. Through her reading and conversations at cohort meetings, she sees she has chosen some activities for which it is proving difficult to show impact on student learning. She also hadn't realized that the significance of an accomplishment needed to be about *her* rather than the students, so she must rewrite those sections. No wonder it seems like she repeated herself when writing the significance and impact sections. She has a moment of panic when she realizes she hasn't yet collected any documentation for her accomplishments, so she makes a list of types of documentation and people to ask. Jan finds that breaking work into smaller tasks helps keep feelings of being overwhelmed at bay. Spring Break couldn't come soon enough!

Chapter Ten

Getting Feedback and Filling Out Forms

Six Word Memoir: Read, Write, Reflect, Revise, Repeat, Submit. —Nanette, AZ

SELF-ASSESS YOUR ENTRY

By this point, you will be more than anxious to prepare to submit; you'll be ready to be done with it all! But taking the time to self-assess and get feedback can make a measurable difference. If a candidate I met recently had done this for her Entry 4, she might have realized that she skipped the significance prompt on two accomplishments, which lowered her score considerably. Give yourself the gift of time and finish early enough so that you can do justice to this last crucial step. Use these self-feedback strategies before mailing your portfolio.

What Works: Using National Board Documents

The Five Core Propositions and the Standards in Your Entries

- Use some standards-based vocabulary and examples, but don't quote large passages.
- Color-code the standard references in your writing.
- Check that you have evidence for *every standard* listed for a particular entry.

The Architecture of Accomplished Teaching (AAT)

- Show evidence of this structure when you describe your lesson sequences.
- The prompts in Entries 1, 2, and 3 generally follow the AAT.

Entry Instructions

- Connect information in the Instructional Context to other sections of your entry.
- Check that you've responded to every prompt.
- Use description, analysis, and reflection in appropriate proportions.
- Comply with all formatting instructions.
- Cite specifics when analyzing the student work samples and videos.
- Adhere to all guidelines concerning names, pagination, margins, and fonts.

The Scoring Guide: Level 4 Rubrics

- Match evidence in your Written Commentary with each bullet in the Level 4 rubric.
- Compare the rubric levels to understand the nuances and differences.
- Make your case with evidence that is clear, consistent, and convincing.

Evaluation of Evidence Guide

- This document describes the aspects of teaching from the Standards used for scoring.
- Assessors have this beside them as they score each entry.
- The links between the parts of your evidence are logical, accurate, and complete.

Why It Works

These documents will help you build a solid wall of evidence. They are the same documents assessors use when scoring, and they provide a road map for candidates.

What Works: Reviewing Your Writing

- Writing should be to the point. Stuff the fluff; it takes up space and contains no evidence.
- Use all three styles of writing, with the smallest proportion being description. There is little or no evidence in description.
- Use active-voice verbs. Eliminate helping verbs and *–ing* forms as far as possible.
- Restate the prompt if you have space to be sure it is answered completely.
- Use some buzzwords (key words) from the standards, but don't overdo them.
- Explain acronyms and abbreviations in your writing.
- Highlight each example in the Written Commentary as you proofread. Doing this will help you gauge how specific you've been.
- Keep the evidence factual, not emotional.
- Use "I" statements that explain your actions. Don't be invisible!
- Use the "Ten Editing Tips" in Appendix Figure 10.1 to trim space without losing content.

Why It Works

These tips support clear, convincing, and consistent writing to satisfy the Level 4 rubric.

What Works: Involving Others

Ask others to read for these factors:

Entry 4 —Read for Question Content. The reader looks at the key questions and prompts and looks for fully developed responses. Look for these:

- *What Is the Nature of the Activity or Accomplishment?* This question needs descriptive writing. The response should be short, clear, and specific.
- *Why Is This Activity or Accomplishment Significant?* This requires analytical writing.
- Check to see that the significance section is about *you* as a teacher and educator, your grade level, your school, and/or your district.

- *What Is the Impact on Student Learning?* Use analytical and reflective writing to connect the accomplishments to student learning. Check to see that the impact section is about the *students*.

All Entries: Read for Standards Content. The reader identifies evidence of the Standards.

- Give the reader the correlating Standards for an entry and make a numbered list of them.
- Ask the reader to place the Standard numbers in the margin as they are identified, or color-code the Standards' evidence.
- When finished, go back through and see if any Standards are missing and find a way to insert evidence if needed.

Read for Understanding and Clarity. The reader sees if they have a clear mental picture of what is being explained.

- Look for terms, acronyms, or programs that are unfamiliar or need further explanation.
- Pay attention to the sequence of events and check to see that things aren't repeated.
- Ask, "Can I picture the lesson or activity being explained?"

Read for Conventions. The reader edits for grammar, sentence structure, active-voice verbs, and word choice.

- Get a "grammar guru" to be the one to check for active voice verbs. This person will love hunting down those passive-voice verbs, *–ing* verbs, and verbs with a helper. Highlighting will make them pop out. Tell this reader to be ruthless.
- Ask this person to check for personal identifying information such as last names, school name, city, or state.

Why It Works

Involving others gives you the opportunity to review your work through another set of eyes. Others may see your writing more clearly than you do.

Important! The final decisions as to what to include, delete, or re-word are yours and yours alone. The entries you submit must reflect *your* teaching practice and *your own thinking*.

FILLING OUT THE FORMS: IMPORTANT DETAILS

Candidates are surprised to discover that finishing the Written Commentary doesn't mean the writing is finished. Indeed, there is a host of additional forms that require filling out, and candidates often forget about them until the last minute. An efficient plan is to fill out the required forms for each entry as soon as you finish the Written Commentary so they are ready when you put the entry together. Another strategy is to fill out a few forms every time you are faced with writer's block or have a pause in your productivity.

The *Electronic Submission at a Glance* for your certificate area illustrates what must be included with each entry. Pay diligent attention to *all* of the graphics. Any missing piece will result in either a delay in processing your entry or portfolio or an inability to score it. Some forms are submitted "as is," and some require additional information to be written or checked. Look at each form carefully to be sure it is completed as required.

Here is a general sampling of forms to be turned in with your portfolio that will require your attention. *Some certificates will have forms not listed here, and some forms listed won't pertain to all certificates—check your certificate directions!*

- Contextual Information Sheet(s)
- Assignment/Prompt/Student Work Cover Sheet(s)
- Classroom Layout Forms
- Instructional Materials Cover Sheets
- Accomplishment Cover Sheet
- Verification Forms where applicable

Check your directions for forms that are particular to your certificate.

What Works

Double and triple check that you've found and filled out all forms needed for your certificate area.

Why It Works

Each form has a specific purpose within the National Board assessment process. Having all forms properly filled out ensures that your portfolio will be complete, and there will be less chance of any kind of glitch occurring.

CANDIDATE VIGNETTES

April: Crunch Time!

Lynn

Lynn missed the April 1 submission deadline she set for herself by a week. She gives herself a short break after completing the writing of the entries, then starts the process of submitting electronically. Using the Electronic Submission at a Glance for her certificate area, Lynn goes down the list for each entry and uploads each file onto the National Board portal. Sometimes this is a slow process, taking much longer than she expected, but eventually it gets done. The uploads include additional forms such as Classroom Layouts and Contextual Information documents. She has a few glitches and scares, but on tax day, April 15, Lynn submits. She is the first in her cohort to submit.

Rick

April is not a good month. Rick has work to do on all four entries. In April there is a death in the family which calls him out of town for a week. It's also the month he and his family plan to visit several colleges with his son, which takes up every weekend. As a result, he has to put in several hours each school night after team practice to write, edit, and revise. It's hard to find time to go to his monthly cohort meeting, and as usual, he shares little. Back in September, Rick thought he could easily finish everything in plenty of time, but as May approaches, he wonders if he will finish on time. He knows he will have to rush the writing on some entries.

Jan

A panic situation! Jan's laptop is stolen from her car. This is the computer she used that day to work on an entry. Fortunately, except for the work done that day, she had played it safe, saving her work on a flash drive and sending her work to her school computer, so she only has to re-create a few hours of work instead of everything. Spring is a busy time for Jan at school and home, and she has trouble again finding time to work. Her son's sports schedule is hectic, it's time for the school Spring Fling she is chairperson of, and the District Committee she serves on has extra meetings. Although she's collected work samples, she hasn't yet selected the students to feature or started any analysis or writing. Finally, Jan throws her hands up and makes the choices needed for Entry 1. She also still needs to work on the video analysis for both Entries 2 and 3. She feels she rushed through these entries and fears she'll have little time for revisions. She works steadily over her Spring Break and makes progress but doesn't finish yet.

Chapter Eleven

Writing at the Assessment Center

Six Word Memoir: Much to say . . . So little time. —Samantha, New York

SHOW WHAT YOU KNOW: THE PURPOSE OF THE ASSESSMENT CENTER EXERCISES

When the frantic race to finish the entries and submit them by the deadline is finally over, candidates heave a collective sigh of relief. However, one last, shadowy obstacle is left looming: the mysterious Assessment Center. While the portfolio is all about your teaching practice—what you *do*—the Assessment Center examines what you *know* about your content as outlined in the NBPTS Standards.

The Assessment Center exercises have evolved since their inception. Originally this examination portion of National Board Certification lasted an entire day and consisted of eight timed tests. Currently the exam has six exercises, lasts four hours, and covers a teacher's knowledge of content and pedagogical knowledge. The portfolio accounts for 80 percent of a candidate's total score and the Assessment Center accounts for 20 percent. Being an accomplished teacher implies mastery of your disciplinary content, so the Assessment Center exercises:

- Focus on knowledge of *content and curriculum* across facets of your discipline.
- Focus on themes, ideas, and principles that represent core concepts and curriculum within a discipline.
- Ask you to demonstrate content knowledge with responses to six exercises developed and designed by practicing professionals in your certificate area.
- Cover the entire age range of the certificate.
- Allow you to show knowledge of developmentally appropriate content across the full spectrum of your certificate.

THE NATURE OF THE EXERCISES AND THE PROMPTS

The nature of the exercises and prompts in the Assessment Center exercises varies among certificates but follows some general patterns. All demand knowledge of content; some also link content knowledge to pedagogy.

EC/MC Generalist, EC/MC Literacy, Reading/Language Arts, EC/YA Exceptional Needs Specialist

These certificates link content to pedagogy. Knowing *how* to teach the concept *is* the content. The exercises ask the candidate to:

- Analyze student responses to a stimulus or topic.
- Analyze, identify, and interpret student misconceptions and errors about a topic.
- Describe thorough, detailed, and appropriate instructional strategies and materials to correct misconceptions and/or extend understanding of the topic.
- Plan worthwhile goals and a developmentally appropriate instructional sequence, based on the Architecture of Accomplished Teaching, that will accomplish the goals.
- Integrate another subject into the instruction.
- Provide a thorough, detailed, and appropriate rationale to justify decisions.

AYA/Science, AYA/Mathematics, EA/Social Studies—History

These certificates have exercises that emphasize connections between specialty areas and another context within the discipline as well as your breadth of knowledge across the disciplines. Pedagogy is less important than your depth and breadth of content knowledge.

- Science certificates allow candidates to choose their area of specialty.
- Math certificates have exercises that address specific areas including algebra, calculus, discrete mathematics, geometry, statistics and data analysis, and technology.
- The Social Studies–History certificate asks you to demonstrate the breadth of your knowledge using graphics and documents in the areas of U.S. history, world history, political science, economics, and geography.
- EA certificates may contain pedagogy.

World Languages Other Than English (WLOE)

- Candidates use a separate room at the Assessment Center suitable for the oral component that is recorded at a computer.
- Candidates compose answers in a separate response booklet.

Music

- Candidates choose a specialty area of band, orchestra, or vocal music.
- Exercises are geared to a performing area.
- Some exercises feature aural material.
- Some exercises require candidates to write musical notation in a lined response booklet provided at the Assessment Center.

These are just a few examples to illustrate the nature of the exercises and prompts found in various certificate areas. The *Assessment at a Glance* document found in the Scoring section of each certificate contains detailed information about the prompts for that certificate. This information guide is crucial for your preparation for the Assessment Center exercises.

The *Assessment at a Glance* contains selected exercises that were administered in a *previous cycle*. You'll find the same information that some past candidates saw on their screen at the Assessment Center. They include instructions for using the computer, stimulus materials where applicable, and the prompts to respond to. These are called *retired prompts,* and they are *not* the same ones you'll see when you take your Assessment Center exercises.

Appendix Figure 11.1 contains further examples, and Appendix Figure 11.2 is a blank form for your own use. Notice that the prompts are multi-part. A common error at the Assessment Center is not scrolling through the entire list of prompts, thus leaving a prompt unanswered. An unanswered prompt earns no score, so pay particular attention to this detail. Other elements of the prompts to pay attention to include:

Table 11.1. Selected *Retired* Assessment Center Exercise "Nutshells"

Certificate	Exercise	Stimulus	Scoring Criteria
ECGEN	#2 Mathematics	Math problem w/error	Identify misconception/difficulty State prerequisites needed Plan an instructional strategy Choose materials/resources Provide rationale for choices
MCGEN	#1 Reading Skills	Transcript of student's oral reading	Identify two patterns of error Cite examples from the text Plan two strategies to address errors Provide rationale for each choice
ECMC/LRLA	#3 Emergent Literacy	Student Writing Sample	Identify one strength/one weakness Tell developmental characteristics Plan two strategies to further skills Provide rationale for each strategy
AYA/Science	#5 Connections in Science (Biology)	Topic Studied in Biology	Explain concepts to biology Connect topic to chemistry Describe student misconceptions Plan strategy to correct the error
ECYA/ENS	#5 Health/PE/Leisure	Student Profile	Discuss one example in each area that student is affected. Design one goal for each area Design two activities to reach goals
EA/ELA	#6 Teaching Writing	Scenario, Student Prompt Student Response	Identify two weaknesses in conventions Identify/analyze one weakness in content or organization Plan two strategies to address weaknesses Explain when to apply strategies Provide rationale for strategies

- Each begins with an active verb such as *identify, plan, design, connect, describe, cite,* or *provide,* telling exactly what you must do to show your knowledge of content and/or pedagogy.
- Each connects to one or more steps on the Architecture of Accomplished Teaching.

The *Criteria for Scoring* rubric included on the Introduction screen for each exercise explains the evidence you must provide. Your response must show clear, consistent, and convincing evidence of each part of the prompts. The Level 4 rubric in your *Scoring Guide* also contains scoring information. So how can you prepare for this daunting task?

THE ARCHITECTURE OF ACCOMPLISHED TEACHING (AAT) AND THE ASSESSMENT CENTER EXERCISES

Earlier I discussed this important document that outlines steps connected to the Five Core Propositions that accomplished teachers use when planning lessons. The Assessment Center exercises may not follow it exactly, but parts of the AAT are embedded in some of the exercises.

The Assessment Center Exercises for *Early Childhood, Middle Childhood,* and *Early Adolescent* certificates often use Steps 1, 2, and 3 as the framework of the exercise.

- Step 1: Knowledge of students is often contained in the stimulus provided. Using the stimulus, the exercise will usually ask you to identify a problem or misconception. In the *SSTARS* acronym; this corresponds to *S* = *S*tudents.
- Step 2: Setting high, worthwhile goals: S*S*TARS = *S*et goals and objectives
- Step 3: Teach using appropriate, effective strategies: SS*T*ARS = *T*each

Note: This will be less applicable for middle or high school teachers because those certificates tend to emphasize content knowledge over pedagogy.

What Works: Strategies for Success at the Assessment Center

- Study! Refresh your knowledge with current information in your content area by reading journals, textbooks, and teacher manuals that span the age spectrum of your certificate.
- Secondary teachers may find retired Advanced Placement/PRAXIS test prompts useful.
- Use the Assessment Center On-line Tutorial on the NBPTS website. This will provide valuable practice and familiarize you with procedures.
- Know the steps on the AAT and be able to apply them to lesson planning. SSTARS is an acronym for the steps on the AAT.
- Make up your own prompts for additional practice.
- Try practicing with different age groups within your certificate area.
- Analyze the exercise directions. Pay attention to these elements:

    Content Area . Reading, math, science, social studies, and so on
    Prompt Materials . A scenario, a stimulus piece, a document
    Action Words . Identify, cite, describe, provide a rationale
    The Task . Show knowledge of . . . , analyze student errors, give examples of . . .

- Scroll down first! Don't spend the entire time responding to one prompt only to find there are other parts you've missed.

- Read the *whole* exercise. There are often several parts to it—each requiring a response.
- Budget your time. 30 minutes for three prompts = 10 minutes for each prompt.
- Practice responding to prompts using a timer set for 30 minutes. Keep practicing. You'll get faster each time. This will help you adjust to responding to a timed test.
- Answer each exercise or prompt completely before moving on. Address all of the parts.
- Once you click on SUBMIT, you cannot return to the exercise. Unanswered prompts earn no points!
- Use the Level 4 rubric for each exercise. Study the rubric and be sure you understand each and every word in it. Construct your responses to satisfy the Level 4 rubric.

What Works: Writing Strategies for Success

- Start with the main points, then go back and fill in details.
- If you get stumped, restart by restating the question as the beginning of your response to jog your memory.
- Using bullets is ok—there are no page limits to constrain your space.
- Match the prompts with your answers. If the prompt asks for goals, your response must have goals.
- Emphasize standards, student achievement, and real-world applications where valid.
- Skip introductions and conclusions. You do *not* have to write in paragraphs.
- Include factual and statistical details you know to be true and accurate.
- Cite examples where you are able. Illustrated evidence is strong evidence.
- Formulate and utilize cause-and-effect information where possible. This exemplifies higher level reasoning skills.
- Be firm in your opinions. Don't say "I think . . ." or "It may be possible . . ." Phrases like these weaken the discussion.
- Write what you already know, and address possible misconceptions.

Why It Works

Knowing what to expect, how to prepare, and how to write responses will lower your anxiety and boost your confidence. You'll do better if you feel ready.

What Works: More Tips for Assessment Center Success

- Take the Assessment Center exercises when you feel you ready. Many candidates share that if they give themselves some time off after completing the portfolio, they have a block of time to focus on the Assessment Center and feel less frazzled and more confident. When the deadline was March 31, candidates had ample down-time to prepare. Submitting well before the May 31 deadline will give you the prep time you need.
- Choose and confirm a date as early as you can after paying your fees. This will give you the greatest choice of dates and will help with your long-range planning.
- Confirm your appointment at least a week ahead of time.
- Read all instructions carefully so you will know exactly what to take: ID, authorizations, supplies, bar codes, and so on.
- Dress in layers in case the room is hot or cold, and take the breaks offered.
- Take a test drive to the assessment center ahead of your testing day. It will give you peace of mind to know where you are going and how long it will take to get there.

- Take the tutorial offered before starting the testing. It will familiarize you with the format and layout of the screen. Especially practice scrolling, as each exercise contains several prompts and you may need to scroll down to see all of the parts.

Why It Works

With purposeful planning, you can approach the Assessment Center with confidence. Use what you already know about accomplished teaching practices to show what you know about your subject-specific content.

What Works: Using Assessment Center Internet Resources

- www.nbpts.org has many resources including certificate standards, scoring rubrics, the *Assessment at a Glance* document, and retired prompts. All of these provide important information to help you prepare. You can also access the Pearson Assessment Center tutorials and information from this site.
- www.ecgen.org is useful to ECGens, MCGens, and Literacy candidates. There are forums for each entry and for Assessment Center exercises. This site also hosts weekly live chats and has an extensive library and archives. Information here is reliable and informative. There is a fee to access this site, but it is worth the cost.
- Yahoo Groups: a number of certificate areas have chat boards here that cover all aspects of the certification process. www.groups.yahoo.com/name of group.
- Google these terms: *NBPTS Assessment Center Power Point* and *NBPTS Assessment Center Exercises* for more sites and resources.

Why It Works

Using a variety of resources will broaden your understanding of the Assessment Center intent and content—all the better to prepare you to do your best.

CANDIDATE VIGNETTES

May: Assessment Center Countdown

Lynn

While others struggle to finish, Lynn can relax a bit in May and start preparing for the Assessment Center. She sometimes has second thoughts about what she submitted but knows no changes can be made now. She must be content with her work. Lynn creates "nutshells" about her Assessment Center exercises using the information found in the Assessment Center at a Glance and the Level 4 rubric. She also does some research on topics and levels she doesn't frequently teach so she'll be ready if any of them show up in the exercises.

Rick

Although the National Board began accepting submissions in April, Rick hasn't been close to being ready. He works long hours in May editing and polishing the four entries, finishing about the middle of the month. He has never let his CSP read any of his entries for feedback, so he can only hope he was on the right track with them. Finishing the entries is a relief, but he now faces uploading everything and still had numerous forms to fill out. This turns out to be enormously time consuming—taking the better part of two days. Rick finally pushes the SUBMIT button on May 20. Now the Assessment Center looms ahead.

Jan

Although the National Board began accepting portfolio submissions on April 1, Jan wasn't ready to upload and submit until almost the end of May. She had to nag some colleagues and a parent for the letters of documentation they promised. The parent hasn't come through, and she decides to use a verification form instead. She hadn't saved her work in files so it took several hours to scan documents and organize materials on her computer. It also took several hours to upload everything. At first she couldn't locate the voucher numbers needed to start the submission process and had to call the 1-800 National Board number. Nothing went smoothly. However, on May 30 she clicks the submission button. It is both a relief and nerve-wracking to send her work into cyberspace. She quickly receives an email notice that her work was received. Now all that's left is the Assessment Center.

Chapter Twelve

Candidate Care

Six Word Memoir: How did I gain 20 pounds? —Susan, Kentucky

TAKING CARE OF YOURSELF

If you are reading this at the beginning of your candidacy, you may wonder why there is a chapter devoted to this topic. If you are well into your candidacy or near the end, you may now recognize the need to take care of yourself and wish you had realized or admitted it sooner. Going through the National Board Certification process is labor intensive, time consuming, and brain challenging—factors that can take a toll on your mental and physical well-being. But no matter where you are in the process, it's never too late to take positive action.

GAIN THE GIFT OF TIME—*JUST FOR THIS YEAR*

Doing some groundwork early in your candidacy can save much stress and frustration later. Your most precious resource will be time: time to think, time to plan, time to write.

What Works

Here are the top four ideas that can ferret out the valuable time you'll need:

- Ask for Support from Your Family. *Just for this school year* delegate some jobs that you've always done yourself. Can the kids fold the laundry and change their own beds? Can your spouse regularly take the kids on an outing during a weekend afternoon so you can have an uninterrupted block of writing time? Can someone other than you be responsible for keeping the house picked up? Can you assign each person one room? Could your spouse help with the grocery shopping once a week or bathe the baby?
- Ask for Support at School. *Just for this school* year ask your principal to let you off the hook of serving on major committees. Most candidates are active members of their school community and often take leadership roles that are time consuming. Too many meetings will eat away at the time you need for planning and writing your entries. Explain that you will need 200–400 hours beyond the school day to work on your entries and that being excused from committees *just for this year* would be an amazing help. Promise you'll be back!

- Find a National Board Support Group, Cohort, or Buddy. *Just for this school year* make meeting with other candidates a priority. Join a support group and attend regularly if such cohorts are offered in your district. You'll have an NBCT facilitator who can guide you through the process, and you'll meet other candidates you can work with, share with, and sympathize with. And they can do the same for you—it's a "you scratch my back and I'll scratch yours" kind of symbiotic arrangement that is mutually beneficial. *Look at surrounding districts* if there is no formal cohort in your district. I've never heard of a cohort that turned down someone who wanted to participate. Most groups meet monthly, so even if it involves a drive, it will likely be worth the effort. *Find a buddy*—a fellow candidate in your district or one who lives near enough to meet with periodically. To find one, look up National Board Certification in your state and ask for a list of candidates. Plan to meet both online frequently and in person at least monthly the first semester and more often as the deadline nears. *Go online.* Several certificate areas have Yahoo online sites where you can find others pursuing your certificate. There are also sites such as Proteacher.com and Teachers.net that serve as a forum for all certificate areas. Review Chapter 3 for a comprehensive list of online sites. Just a word of caution: *Never send your work to someone you don't know!* If someone plagiarizes your work, there could be negative consequences for both you and the plagiarizer.
- Find at Least One Weekend or Extended Period of Time Every Month When You Can Have Uninterrupted Work Time. *Just once* plan to give yourself a working retreat—especially in February or March. If someone you know has a cabin or beach house, ask if you can use it. Rent a room at a hotel. Send your family out of town for a weekend so you can have the house to yourself. Be creative to find a way to carve out some extra precious time. Sometimes this can work with a buddy, but only if you can limit conversation and concentrate on *your* needs.

Why It Works

These strategies are proven to boost your efficiency, give you the gift of time, and give you the support and resources you'll need.

PROCRASTINATION: YOUR WORST ENEMY

I alluded to this earlier, but procrastination is seriously the worst judgment error you can make as a National Board candidate—*seriously!* It will do you in faster than most people can lick an ice-cream cone on a summer day. Many believe that they do their best work under pressure. This may actually be true for one or two out of a hundred candidates. But the other 98 who think they work best under pressure are almost always mistaken, at least in this case. Writing a National Board entry is time intensive and cannot be accomplished by pulling an all-nighter— or even two or three. Candidates who score well have usually devoted weeks if not months to planning and writing an entry. They plan and video multiple lessons. They write and revise entries multiple times.

As an NBCT who has facilitated well over a hundred candidates, I can tell you firsthand that procrastination is a devastating habit. It would take many hands to count the number of candidates I've seen who put off reading their standards, put off reading the portfolio instructions, put off planning lessons that met the entry requirements, put off collecting student work samples, put off filming lessons, and put off writing. I've had candidates who admitted in March that they hadn't read their standards yet, read their portfolio instructions yet, nor made a single video. Those candidates did not certify on their first attempt. There is just no way to produce the quality portfolio the National Board expects if one repeatedly and consistently procrastinates.

The fact that I've devoted nearly a full page of text to procrastination should tell you how seriously I regard this as a fatal flaw. You can be the best teacher at your school, but if you don't devote the time and energy to planning and writing, your chances of certifying are slim. There are many reasons teachers don't certify on their first attempt, but please don't let *procrastination* be the reason *you* don't certify. It is an avoidable pitfall.

What Works: Activate! Don't Procrastinate!

Procrastination is inaction. The best thing you can do is to take action—any action. Taking action has many benefits that will serve you well as you work through the process, and it can save you at the end.

Being Proactive: What does being a proactive National Board candidate mean? It means you don't worry and stew for weeks or months before actually *doing* things that need to be done. Consider:

- Read your Standards often and really well. Highlight the examples given in each one to refer to later. NBCTs always tell candidates to read their standards thoroughly and often, and there is a reason for that. You have to know them and show them to certify.
- Read your portfolio entry instructions often and really well. You can't produce lessons that will score well unless you truly know what the entry asks you to do. Ninety-nine percent of what you need to know and do is in your instructions. Period! Get intimate with the instructions!
- Get started on *something*. Find one thing in one entry to start working on. Once you get the ball rolling, it's more likely you'll keep going. The Instructional Context can be a good starting place. Or respond to one prompt—do anything to get started.
- Start writing early. An Instructional Context is a good place to start.
- Get a system in place to organize your entries and materials. Being able to lay your hands on something when you need it will be an enormous help as you go along.
- Set aside a designated work time each week. Stick to it and use it.

Why It Works

Proactive behaviors will keep you on track, raise your confidence level, and produce results that will pay off. Think of yourself as being a sculptor chipping away little by little at the marble. Eventually the sculptor's chipping brings into being a beautiful statue. By chipping away steadily section by section in your instructions, you will produce a fully formed, thoughtful portfolio that documents your accomplished teaching.

PAYING ATTENTION TO YOUR HEALTH

As I mentioned in this chapter's opening paragraph, the National Board Certification process is labor intensive, time consuming, and brain challenging. All of these things take a toll on the body, mind, and spirit, especially during the last three months. But there are things you can do to minimize the effects all this hard work can heap on you.

Your Body

- *Eat Right and Stay Hydrated.* I know—yada, yada, yada. You hear this all the time. But considering that you may be doing more sitting than usual at the computer, keeping the carbs and sugar consumption under control could make a difference in the way you feel. Keep a bottle or glass of water handy at the computer and drink it!
- *Exercise.* Take some walks. Again, yada, yada, yada—but this is another thing that can make a difference. Fit in some short walks, alone if possible. Walking seems to get the juices flowing to your muscles and your brain. I practically wrote some entries in my head while on walks. I seemed to be able to think more clearly and figure out how to get past blocks I was experiencing. Outdoor walks worked best for me when the weather permitted—maybe the noise at the gym competed with the "noise" in my head. And sometimes I didn't want the hassle of going to the gym. Just heading out my door and walking through the neighborhood was what I preferred.
- Another strategy is to move your computer to a counter area so you can stand while working rather than sitting. Standing is more beneficial than sitting. Try it!
- Do some yoga. Get a yoga CD to play when you need a break. It's quiet, calm, and gentle. Most routines last about 30 minutes, but stretching for even 15 minutes will be energizing. You will feel much better, I guarantee.

Your Mind

All of the above will help your state of mind, but try this as well.

- *Positive Self-talk* can work wonders. To combat those feelings that you are going crazy, that you are overwhelmed, and that this is too hard, formulate some positive statements to help you relax. Try incorporating these thoughts into your mind-set:

> I can figure this out.
> I'm doing my best.
> I'll come back to this later.
> I'll answer just one prompt now.
> I know how to do this.
> This is a common feeling for candidates to have.
> I'm not alone in this process.
> I'll slow down and approach one prompt or section at a time.
> I'll read the directions one more time.
> I'll read this standard again.
> I'll ask my buddy, mentor, cohort, or website for support.
> I can adjust my schedule for just today, this week, or until this entry is done.

Your Spirit

Taking care of your physical and mental needs will automatically lift your spirits. As you encounter obstacles, you'll find yourself more resilient and able to rebound. You can recognize that tackling a difficult challenge always involves setbacks and frustrations, but you won't let them derail your efforts. You'll be able to continue on in a more positive frame of mind.

What Works

Planning to care for yourself will help you have the energy you need. You'll have the confidence, stamina, and perseverance to see the challenge through to the end.

Why It Works

Your body will find a way to take a break one way or another. It's much better for *you* to plan the breaks your body will take rather than find yourself ill and unable to work. As a teacher you are already exposed to massive doses of germs from your students, so do all you can to keep yourself healthy—in body, mind, and spirit!

CANDIDATE VIGNETTES

June

Lynn

Lynn schedules her Assessment Center (AC) exercises for June 10. This gives her time after school is out to prepare. She makes a test drive to the testing center during rush hour so she'll know the worst-case scenario when it comes to drive time. She also checks the AC information on the Pearson site so she'll know what she can and cannot bring to the testing center. She hopes her preparation will be enough and that the timed exercises won't be too stressful. She feels some test anxiety but tries to stay calm. At the end, Lynn feels like she did her best and hopes for a good outcome.

Rick

Rick's AC exercises are scheduled for early June. Because he submitted so late in May, he doesn't feel prepared, so he postpones the date until later in the month. He's told they cannot be postponed again because the testing window will close, so he hopes he doesn't get sick or have some other setback. He's tired of the whole process but makes an effort to figure out what might be on the exercises. On test day, he leaves mildly hopeful that he did well enough. He ran out of time on one exercise but completed the other five within the 30 minutes.

Jan

What was she thinking when she scheduled her AC tests for only three days after school let out? She never dreamed she'd submit so late and close to the deadline. There is so much to do at the end of the school year, and she has little time to study. She intends to make "nutshells" of each exercise but runs out of time. She looks over her Scoring Guide and the retired prompts in the Assessment at a Glance document but feels totally unprepared when she goes to the testing center. The security procedures create anxiety, and she isn't sure she can concentrate enough to do well. When she leaves the center, her mind is a blank—she just feels relieved that she can get back to having a life.

Chapter Thirteen

Top 10 Confusing Topics and FAQs

Six Word Memoir: A PhD without the Stat class. —Claudia, OK

WHAT DOES THIS MEAN?

Every year and in every certificate area candidates seem to struggle with similar sets of challenges within the process. Especially as the deadline approaches, websites and chat rooms that focus on National Board Certification light up with frantic requests for clarification. Part of the issue stems from the language in the portfolio directions. Prompts are written to give candidates the broadest range of possibilities, which is a double-edged sword. It means that there are fewer limitations placed on pedagogy, for example. But the lack of specificity may contribute to difficulty deciphering "what the National Board wants" or "what the assessors expect to see." Some terms used are National Board jargon and may not be familiar to all. And finally, the prompts are often long and contain multiple parts that must be addressed. Here are the top 10 topics that candidates bring up again and again, along with *fabricated, abbreviated* examples to clarify each.

Overarching Goal(s), Objectives, and Activities

Most certificates have one or more prompts that ask you to explain these elements of your lesson sequence plan.

Overarching Goal

This is the biggest idea, concept, or understanding you want students to take away from the unit of study. It is something that can cut across a variety of areas of a topic and may be difficult to measure. Example: *The students will understand that there are a variety of ways to organize and interpret information about people, places, and environments.*

Goal

This is another broad understanding of a topic, but slightly more specific than the overarching goal. It is still conceptual; the learning may be difficult to measure, and it is articulated with the word "understand." Example: *The students will understand that maps interpret physical and man-made features.* The verb used in goal statements often comes from one of the higher levels of Bloom's Taxonomy and needs to be more conceptual than concrete.

Objective

The objective describes the specific, measurable learning(s) you want to occur within a particular lesson. Example: *The students will identify physical and man-made features on a map.* The verb(s) used in the objective statement may come from one of the lower levels of Bloom's Taxonomy, is relatively concrete, and articulates a student action to be taken. Objectives can be evaluated.

Activity

This is what the students do to learn or practice the objective. Example: *Students will construct or draw a map that includes physical and man-made features.* When the activity is completed, the teacher will be able to assess whether or not students learned the objective. Notice the concrete, active-voice verb used to construct the statement.

   Be very careful not to plan a lesson sequence or unit of study based mainly on activities. It is important that the goals and objectives are planned first. Plan the activities last. Otherwise the goal(s) and objective(s) may not be tightly connected.

Nature and Flow

This is a brief description of what a lesson sequence or unit is about and the general order of lessons.

Nature

Generally, what is this lesson sequence about? Example: *This is a unit on force and motion that explores Newton's three Laws of Motion.*

Flow

This refers to the general order of the lessons so that assessors can "see" the unit at a glance. Example: *I began the unit by showing a video about how force affects the motion of objects. Each lesson in sequence presented one of Newton's Laws of Motion. Within each lesson I presented instruction using direct instruction. Then students did hands-on activities using ramps to demonstrate the laws, which sometimes took multiple days to complete. Within each lesson, students took notes in their science journal, worked in a group to conduct inquiry investigations, recorded the tests and results, and wrote a reflection of their new learning. The culminating activity consisted of building roller-coaster-type ramps that each group then explained and demonstrated to the class. I assessed them using a student- and teacher-created rubric.* The idea here is to give the assessor a general sense of how the lessons progressed, not a blow-by-blow, day-by-day recounting of each and every lesson in the unit.

Instructional Context and Contextual Information

The very names of these documents guarantee a mix-up. They are like kissing cousins—which is which? They have elements in common but aren't really the same.

Instructional Context (IC)

This document is about your class. This is the first section of your Written Commentary in Entries 1, 2, and 3. It gives the assessor a snapshot of your class and your teaching situation (context). Conditions and students you highlight here need to be referenced again in the Written Commentary. While the questions are the same for Instructional Context in all three entries, your responses will not be identical because either you are addressing a different subject for each or a different aspect of your subject for each. So a Literacy candidate is addressing the students taught for writing, reading and speaking, and listening and viewing; an MCGen candidate is addressing writing, social studies, and science; and a middle school Math teacher is addressing mathematical thinking and reasoning, mathematical discourse, and small-group mathematical collaborations. For all certificates, the groups used for each entry may or may not be the same.

Contextual Information (CI)

These documents are about your school and possibly your district. Here you describe any special programs you teach under, state mandates, type of community your school or district is located in, and your access to technology. You need one for each of Entries 1, 2, and 3, and if your entry features students from more than one school, you'll need one for each school. If you have more than one school, label one as "A" and one as "B" and refer to them that way.

Instructional Materials

Instructional Materials (IMs) are items used or produced during a teaching sequence. They allow assessors to better understand the activity in your video or Written Commentary. They are not scored separately but are considered a part of your entry. They may be submitted in the same form in which they are presented to the class. The National Board FAQ section states that IMs may be samples of student work unless otherwise specifically stated in the entry. Choose IMs that help the assessor know about the teaching you did, the content you covered, and/or enrichment or remediation—things that help the assessor to gain a more complete picture of your lesson.

Organization of Accomplishments in Entry 4

This is discussed extensively in Chapter 8, but it causes so much confusion I'll tackle it here too. There are basically three ways to organize your accomplishments: (1) with Learner, Leader, Collaborator, and Family Involvement headings; (2) with an "umbrella" heading; or (3) as individual accomplishments. One style is not better than another. Which you choose depends largely on how you think and write.

Learner, Leader, Collaborator, and Family Involvement Headings

If you choose this way, then you discuss the important things you've done under each heading. "Learner" may include workshops and trainings. "Leader" might showcase activities in which you were the organizer or presenter. "Collaborator" will include times you worked with others to achieve a goal, and "Family Involvement" will include your Communication Log as well as other important interactions such as a family math night. For each event, committee, or topic you use, you must tell why it was significant (to you, your grade level, your school) and how it impacted student learning.

Umbrella Headings

This works well when you see patterns in your accomplishments. You might title a heading "Literacy" and list workshops and trainings, family literacy events you've organized, or committees you've served on to promote this topic. Again, for each you list you must discuss how these show you as a learner, leader, or collaborator and explain the significance and impact on student learning.

Individual Accomplishments

Here you use each activity as an accomplishment and tell which category(ies) this accomplishment addresses. Examples might include "Technology," "Parent Math Night," or "Overnight Science Camp" as headings. As with the other styles, you'll need to tell which category(ies) each addresses and explain the significance and impact on student learning.

   Choose activities with the biggest bang for the buck—strong impact on student learning and, where possible, activities that address more than one category. For example, if you took training and then shared the information with your staff, that activity would show you as both learner and leader.

Formatting and Editing

Both of these figure large in producing your final entry copies. Page limits demand clear, concise writing, which is always a challenge. You cannot exceed the page limits. At the end of the maximum number of pages allowed, the assessors simply stop reading. It is a good idea to stick as closely as possible to the suggested page limits give for each section of an entry. The National Board knows approximately how much space is needed for well-crafted responses. If you write far less or far more, you are probably either leaving out important evidence or adding fluff.

Formatting

Your portfolio instructions give very specific formatting specifications that must be followed exactly. The basics include using 12 point, Times New Roman font, double-spacing, and 1 inch margins. But each certificate and each entry within certificates have specifications particular to that entry, so my best advice is to read and re-read those instructions. There can be issues such as margins that print with 1 inch borders on one printer but not another to deal with. My advice is to find a printer that produces the margins you need and use it.

Editing

Most candidates start the writing process by writing everything they can think of, the natural consequence of which is that some serious editing needs to take place. Here are 10 tips for editing:

- Use active-voice verbs. Eliminate *–ing* forms and helping verbs. *plan, create . . .*
- Use "I" in statements with an active verb. *I organized . . . , I taught*
- Indent paragraphs two or three spaces instead of five spaces.
- Use one space between sentences.
- Eliminate *that, the, this,* and *my* as often as possible. This rarely changes the meaning of the sentence.
- Turn on automatic hyphenation.

- Turn off widows and orphans.
- Start your text on the same line as a heading. *Instructional Context: The class featured in this entry* . . .
- Don't repeat yourself! Saying something once is enough.
- Eliminate adjectives and adverbs where possible.

See Appendix Figure 10.1, "Ten Editing Tips," for even more ideas.

Using Names/Identification in Entry 4

Unlike the other entries that want complete anonymity, the assessors need to know the identity of the people who are verifying the claims in your accomplishments. So in general, it's ok to leave in the names of people and places, including your school, district, and so forth. Always email or call 1-800-22TEACH for specific clarification.

Other Confusing Terms

National Board terminology is often different from the everyday terms used by teachers across the country, and that often leads to confusion.

- *Instructional/Lesson Sequence.* A series of related lessons and/or activities that support a common goal or theme. It is not limited to a single lesson or activity. Example: *A lesson sequence on force and motion.*
- *Unit.* Part of an academic course focusing on a selected theme or concept. A unit may also refer to a chapter in a curriculum text.
- *Featured Lesson.* The lesson shown on a video or from which student work samples were derived.
- *Evidence.* Accomplished teaching *examples* or student *actions* that have a strong foundation in fact, would be convincing to most people, and would not be easily disproved by interpretation. Assessors want to know that you recognized evidence and used them in your teaching. Example: *When he said . . . , I knew that he misunderstood the concept. So I referred him back to the graphic organizer. I knew she had trouble tracking print left to right so I . . .*
- *Small-group Discussion.* Used in videos to show how a teacher facilitates interactions among students. Generally it is a group of three to five students although the numbers may vary according to specific entry directions.
- *Whole-class Discussion.* Used in videos to show the teacher effectively engaging the entire class as a group. There should be evidence of interactions with individual students but not every student. However, it should be clear that the whole class is actively engaged in the discussion.

The last two confusing topics pertain to ECGen and MCGen candidates. EA/EAYA Science candidates have a requirement called Major Ideas of Science which is related yet particular to the two science certificates and not discussed here. Science candidates should read and follow the instructions in their own certificate.

Unifying Concepts/Big Idea of Science

This is an ECGen and MCGen requirement for Entry 3 that many teachers struggle with. It is the "lens" through which lessons are planned and needs to be chosen before planning the unit.

That way the lessons will lead students toward the conceptual understandings that underlie the unifying concept. These concepts are often principles or patterns that cut across strands of science in ways that help students organize and comprehend. The five unifying concepts identified in your National Board portfolio are:

- *Systems, Order, and Organization (SOO).* Nature is made up of many systems that are related or connect in some way. A system is a whole that is composed of parts arranged in an orderly manner according to some plan or function. Nature is composed of many inter-related systems.
- *Evidence, Models, and Explanation (EME).* Models are used to represent things that may be difficult to see or measure. Nature behaves in predictable ways, and searching for explanations is an important function of science. Nature if predictable, and we can use evidence and models to develop explanations to understand our world. This is a difficult concept for young children to grasp.
- *Change, Constancy, and Measurement (CCM).* The natural world is constantly changing. Children may observe the changes in position and apparent shape of the moon. The height of ramps can be changed to affect the distance an object travels. Some things remain constant, such as the length of time it takes the earth to rotate around the sun or keeping the surface of a ramp the same through a series of tests. Measurements can document changes and consistency over time. Nature is constantly changing, but many repeating patterns are constant.
- *Evolution and Equilibrium (EE).* There is a great deal of diversity in nature, yet all organisms have particular characteristics. From one generation to another, nature selects and adapts characteristics (evolution) that provide advantages for survival. Natural systems tends to be balanced (in equilibrium) over time.
- *Form and Function (FF).* There is a relationship between the form (what it looks, sounds, feels, and smells like) of an object and its function (what it does). Children can learn that the form of a bird's beak determines what it eats or that water plants with leaves with bladders attached help the leaf float so it can capture sunlight for photosynthesis.

Now let's take a science topic and briefly view it through various unifying concepts in order to see how the focus of a unit of study might look under each.

Topic: Butterflies

SSO: A caterpillar's life cycle (*system*) is *ordered* and *organized* in predictable ways.

EME: Through *models* (stages of a butterfly kit) students can *explain* the *evidence* that caterpillars change into butterflies.

CCM: Characteristics of this species of caterpillar remain *constant*, but the caterpillar will *change* over time, and that change can be *measured*.

EE: Our environment strives for *equilibrium* or balance among living things, but in order to survive, they change over time (*evolution*).

FF: The butterfly has wings (*form*) that makes it possible to fly (*function*), thus enabling it to find food and escape predators.

The above fabricated examples are meant only to demonstrate how the unifying concepts could be applied to a single science topic. They may or may not be appropriate for use in an entry. All unifying concepts and science topics can be tested with inquiry activities, but keep in mind that some lend themselves easier than others to student inquiry, the other important element of this entry, especially considering the limited resources and science training typical of Generalists.

Inquiry Science

In a nutshell, inquiry involves asking a question and devising a test that will give information to answer the question. Inquiry occurs on a continuum from totally teacher directed to totally student directed. Aim for somewhere in the middle for this entry. Start with student questions and their current level of knowledge of a topic, then use what you know about the science content to guide students to ways to test their hypothesis. Inquiry involves having a constant and a variable. In general, for elementary students, having just one variable keeps the focus of the inquiry clear. An abbreviated example of a science inquiry might look something like this:

Unifying Concept: Change, Constancy, and Measurement

Topic: Force and Motion

Student Generated Inquiry Question: Will my car roll further on a ramp with a smooth, bumpy, or slick surface?

Change: Cover the surface of several ramps with different materials to represent smooth, rough, bumpy, and slick surfaces. Students discuss possible surfaces and materials to use and make plans for covering the ramps.

Constants: The height and length of the ramps are the same. Roll the same object down the ramp each time. Place the object at the top of the ramp and hold in position by placing a ruler in front of it so that there is not additional force put upon the object that could skew the results. Use the same unit of measurement for each test. Do three tests with each surface.

Measurement: Measure the distance from the end of the ramp to where the object stops.

Alternate Inquiry Question: Does the surface area of a ramp affect the speed an object travels down the ramp? *Variable:* Measure for speed instead of distance.

Elementary teachers need to research and read about both inquiry and the science content. Comprehensive science information is included at the end of the Generalist portfolio instructions. Websites such as ecgen.org have extensive libraries describing inquiry science, and there is a lot of general information available on the Internet. Please note that the level of inquiry found in many district-mandated science kits may not be up to the level this entry requires. Teachers often have to supplement such kits. It is also imperative that teachers be well-versed in the content science. For example a teacher who wants to use "sink-and-float," a topic included in numerous science kits, needs to understand concepts such as water density and surface tension.

NATIONAL BOARD CERTIFICATION IS RIGOROUS PROFESSIONAL DEVELOPMENT

National Board Certification is meant to be a rigorous process that takes deep thinking and broad knowledge to accomplish. Every certificate has particular challenges, but the entire process challenges teachers to formulate effective learning *for these students, at this time, in this setting.* It is rigorous professional development in the highest form.

Chapter 13

CANDIDATE VIGNETTES

November Score Release: The Results Arrive

Lynn

Lynn was able to forget about scores for most of the summer and fall, but by November she was getting anxious. Relief came on score release day when she logged onto her profile to see her score and she knew she had certified. Her score was 278, and she had done especially well on the Assessment Center exercises. Lynn was now a National Board Certified Teacher.

Rick

The summer flew by, and November came quickly for Rick. He had almost forgotten about the score release. He received an email from the National Board letting him know the score release date. He hadn't thought that he would be worried about getting his scores, but he discovered that he was actually quite nervous. When he opened his profile page, he saw he had certified. Mark earned 275 points, the minimum, but he was extremely happy that he was now a National Board Certified Teacher.

Jan

Jan worried all summer about her scores. She had rushed through several entries and felt she hadn't done well on the Assessment Center exercises because she had so little time to prepare. When Lisa opened her profile page, she saw that her score was 265. This was hugely disappointing news; the thought of doing parts over again was overwhelming. But after a time, she realized that doing one entry and one Assessment Center exercise over could earn her the points she needed, and that seemed manageable. Lisa became a re-take candidate and this time felt much more confident about her efforts. Lisa scored well on her re-take attempt and certified with a score of 280 points, thus becoming a National Board Certified Teacher.

Appendix

STUDENTS (Step 1: Knowledge of Students) WHAT I KNOW ABOUT: • These students at this time, in this setting • Learning styles • Abilities • Needs • Prior knowledge	
SET GOALS (Step 2: Set high, worthwhile goals) • Goals • Objectives • Activities • Unifying Concepts/Big Ideas	
TEACH (Step 3: Implement instruction) • Appropriate strategies • Activities support goals • Appropriate pacing	
ASSESS (Step 4: Evaluate learning in light of the goals) • Monitor progress purposefully • Assess throughout the lesson sequence • Observations • Informal • Formal • Remediate/Enrich	
REFLECT (Step 5: Reflect on student learning) • Effectiveness • Successes • Modifications	
START AGAIN (Step 6: Set new high, worthwhile goals) • For these students, at this time, in this setting	

Figure 2.1 SSTARS Lesson Plan Template

Directions: In the first column write (paraphrase) each bullet in the Level 4 rubric for this entry. In the middle column write the Standard that the rubric bullet corresponds to. In the third column list specific evidence from the video that shows that rubric concept and Standard. The rubric is found in the Scoring Guide, Part 2.

Rubric Bullet Concept Evidence	Entry Standard(s)	Video Examples of Behaviors, Quotes, Actions

Figure 8.1 Finding the Level 4 Rubric in a Video

Appendix

Entry: _____   **Topic:**_____

MINUTE	TEACHER TALK	STUDENT TALK	INTERACTION S/S S/T T/S		EVIDENCE OF PROMPT/RUBRIC BULLET
1:00					
2:00					
3:00					
4:00					
5:00					
6:00					
7:00					
8:00					
9:00					
10:00					
11:00					
12:00					
13:00					
14:00					
15:00					

Student to student
Student to teacher
Teacher to student

Figure 8.2 Analysis of a Video by Minutes

LEARNER	LEADER	COLLABORATOR	PARENT/COMMUNITY
1.	1.	1.	1.
2.	2.	2.	2.
3.	3.	3.	3.
4.	4.	4.	4.
5.	5.	5.	5.
6.	6.	6.	6.
7.	7.	7.	7.
8.	8.	8.	8.
9.	9.	9.	9.
10.	10.	10.	10.

Figure 9.1 Entry 4 Accomplishments Brainstorming List

Appendix

TEACHER :_____

DATE/METHOD	STUDENT	COMMUNICATED WITH	REASON/TOPIC	RESPONSE	OUTCOME

Figure 9.2 Communication Log

Directions: Using your brainstormed list of accomplishments, look for patterns. Put accomplishments together under an "umbrella" heading. Then fill out the remaining boxes with information to address each prompt: the nature of; the significance of; and the impact on student learning.

Accomplishment # _____   TITLE: _____

ACTIVITIES:

The Nature of the Accomplishment: *WHAT is it about? Tell a __LITTLE__; writing should be short and succinct!*

The Significance of the Accomplishment: *SO WHAT? This is about YOU/GRADE LEVEL/SCHOOL. Tell __MORE__.*

The Impact on Student Learning: This is about KIDS! *Give specific examples of each impact cited. Tell __the MOST!__*

Figure 9.3 Entry 4 Accomplishments: Combining Activities

Dear Colleague / Parent,

Thanks for sharing your observation about how my workshop on erasing the whiteboard improved the student performance of this skill in your classroom. Could you take a few minutes and write a note or letter describing how the presentation impacted how you now teach students to erase the whiteboard and what your students learned as a result? Because I need specific information for my National Board entry, I have enclosed some sentence starter *suggestions* below that will make your writing easier. Please limit your letter to one page. Thank you!
Lulu

1. NB Candidate's Name: *Lulu*
2. Date of Presentation: *February 23, 20__*
3. Describe how the workshop impacted your teaching of the skill or concept:

A) In Lulu's workshop, I learned that I can teach my students to erase whiteboards in a new way.

OR

B) Learning to erase white boards the way Lulu showed in her workshop changed the way I teach my students to practice that skill.

OR

C) I saw the impact of what I learned at Lulu's workshop when my students ____. Before I attended Lulu's workshop my students would ___, but now they ____.

OR

D) In past years my students would __, but after this presentation they __, which helps them __. This impacted my students' learning by ___.

Tweak the sentence stems to fit the person writing the letter (colleague, parent, student, etc.). Ask for documentation as early as possible to avoid scrambling for them at the last minute.

Figure 9.4 Documentation Letter Template

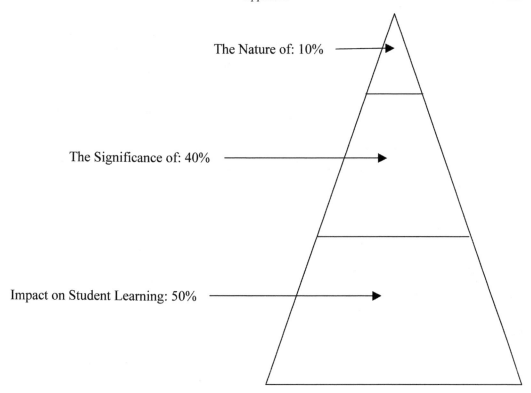

The Nature of: 10%

The Significance of: 40%

Impact on Student Learning: 50%

Figure 9.5 Candy Corn Analogy

Although the significance of any accomplishment is ultimately tied to impact on student learning*, the direct connection for this prompt is about how it was significant to YOU as an educator, or to your grade level, other teachers or important stake-holders, or its effect on your building, district, regional, state or national policy. It shows how you went above and beyond routine expectations.

EXPECTED & ROUTINE VS. ABOVE & BEYOND	WHAT IS THE SIGNIFICANCE?
Accomplishment needs to show important effort. Show the assessor why this is not a routine effort. Detail what you did that was above and beyond.	How does this accomplishment stand out? How is it important to your teaching or learning? How is it more effective than usual in promoting learning?
Assigned committees vs. voluntary committees; Why was your presence important? What did you Bring to the committee that would otherwise be missing? What was your role?	What was the effect on your teaching skills or those of other committee members?
Parent conferences vs. student-led conferences; How were you instrumental in initiating this format at your grade level or school?	What was the effect on instructional practices and/or two-way parent communication?
Required district trainings vs. leading a work-shop using your own expertise.	What effect did the learning you ac-quired have on your own teaching? What effect did the workshop have on other teachers' or stake-holders knowledge, skills and/or abilities?
Membership in a professional organization vs. having a leadership position or giving a presen-tation for members.	What effect did your participation have on educational, building, district, regional, state or national policy or actions?
Attending department or faculty meetings vs. being the chair person or facilitator of meetings.	What was the impact on student learn-Ing? How did you grow? Give specific examples.
Participating in a Parent Open House or Back-to-School Night vs. planning a presentation to en-gage parents/families in their child's learning.	What was the result of your efforts? What effect did it have on the knowledge, skills, And abilities of the stake-holders?

*Student learning can be that of your own students, students of colleagues or adults/colleagues.

Figure 9.6 Entry 4 Significance of an Accomplishment

Tips are based on Microsoft Word documents. Instructions for other systems may differ.

1. **Turn Off "Widow/orphan" Control.** This prevents a single line of a paragraph from being at the top of a new page. You'll save several lines in the space of an entry.
From the "Home" tool bar at the top of a page, Find "Paragraph" >Find the little arrow in bottom right corner > Go to "Line and Page Breaks" > Uncheck to turn off control.

2. **Set to Auto-hyphenate.** This will break words at the ends of lines to properly hyphenate. Saving even a few spaces on each page can help.
Go to the "Page Layout" tool bar. Above "Page Setup" you'll see "Hyphenation." Click on "Automatic" to turn it on.

3. **Use Contractions.** They save several spaces each time you use them. Word has an auto-correct feature called "Find and Replace." You may need to do this for each contraction.
Hit CTRL F > Select "Replace" tab >In "Find" field, type " do not" or the phrase you want to replace > In the "Replace" field type the contraction that fits ("don't") > Click "Replace All."

4. **Don't Spell Out Numbers.** You can break the rule you learned in school. Use numerals such as *12* instead of *twelve* and *6th* instead of *sixth*.

5. **Start Your Commentary on the Same Line as the Heading.** Example:
Video Analysis: This lesson features 89 1st graders learning to sharpen pencils.

6. **Make Sure Your Header with the Candidate Number Is Outside the Margin and Not in the Body.** To avoid this problem, set your header up to align automatically. To do that, go to the *Insert Tool Bar, then click on header > Blank > Type Candidate number in the text box, and then align to the right corner.*

7. **Find and Replace the Period Double Space.** This is another space saver.
Hit CTRL-F > "Find and Replace" tab > In the Find field, hit the space bar twice. In the "Replace" field, hit the space bar once > Click "Replace All."

8. **Take *The, My,* and *That* Out of Most Sentences.** The meaning won't change but you'll gain space. Replace *I collected the papers* with *I collected papers* and *I know that students . . .* with *I know students . . .*

9. **Remove as Many Adjectives and Adverbs as Possible.** Replace *She writes with vivid and inspired word choice . . .* with *She writes with strong word choice . . .*

10. **Indent Paragraphs Two or Three Spaces Instead of Five, *or* Eliminate Paragraphs Altogether If You Are Desperate.** If you choose the latter, try all of the above first, then consider *bolding the first word or two* as a visual aid to the assessor.

Figure 10.1 Ten Editing Tips to Trim Space without Trimming Content

Use the *Assessment at a Glance* document found in the scoring section of the NB website to outline each exercise. Pay attention to the *VERBS* used in the prompts.

IDENTIFY, ANALYZE, INTERPRET, PROVIDE, PLAN, JUSTIFY, RESPOND, ADDRESS, EXAMINE, REFLECT, CREATE, DISCUSS, EXPLAIN, ADAPT, SHOW, CONNECT, DEFINE, CONSTRUCT, SUGGEST, PROPOSE, APPLY, COMPOSE, RECOMMEND, PREDICT, INFER,

CONTENT AREA	VERBS	STIMULUS	TEACHER ACTION
EXERCISE #1: ECGEN Show your ability to analyze and make inferences about a student's reading development. Identify strengths and plan strategy based on strengths. Include resources and rationale for your choices.	analyze infer identify plan strategy include provide rationale	1 student progress report	Identify 2 strengths & rationale 1 Goal Strategy & activities to accomplish goal Resources / materials Rationales
EXERCISE #2: MCGEN Identify math misconception/error. Identify concepts/skills needed for understanding and provide strategies with rationale to assist understanding of the skill/concept.	identify provide	student work	Identify error pattern in problem Identify concepts needed for understanding Provide strategies to correct error Provide rationale for choices
EXERCISE #3: LITERACY Analyze a student writing sample Describe developmental characteristics and propose two strategies to address weakness or build on strengths.	analyze describe	writing sample	1 area of strength 1 area of weakness Describe developmental level in detail Propose 2 appropriate strategies Rationale
EXERCISE #4: AYA/ELA Demonstrate understanding of language development and determine patterns in student's language development. Read a second language learner's oral & written response. Analyze patterns and provide strategies to further student's development.	demonstrate determine read analyze provide	oral and written response to a prompt	1 significant feature of oral language 1 significant feature of written language Analyze language patterns 2 strategies to further student's development
EXERCISE #5: ECYA/ENS Analyze student profile and state how the student would be affected in areas of physical, emotional & social development. Design goals and activities that provide opportunities for success, improved self-image & foster independence.	analyze state design	student profile	Analyze profile State how student is affected Design 2 goals and activities
EXERCISE #6: EAYA/WLOE Demonstrate knowledge of how the target language works. Given 20 errors embedded in excerpts of a variety of texts in the target language, you correct each error and explain why it is an error.	demonstrate correct explain	excerpts from various target language texts.	Find and correct errors embedded in various target language texts and explain why it is an error.

Figure 11.1 Assessment Center Sample Exercise "Nutshells"

Assessment Center Sample Exercise "Nutshell" Blank Template

Use the *Assessment at a Glance* document and the Level 4 rubric found in the *Scoring Guide Part 2* to outline each exercise. Pay attention to the *verbs* used in the prompts.

Identify, analyze, interpret, provide, plan, justify, respond, address, examine, reflect, create, discuss, explain, adapt, show, connect, define, construct, suggest, propose, apply, compose, recommend, predict, infer

CONTENT AREA	VERBS	STIMULUS	TEACHER ACTION
EXERCISE #1:			
EXERCISE #2:			
EXERCISE #3:			
EXERCISE #4:			
EXERCISE #5:			
EXERCISE #6:			

Figure 11.2 Assessment Center Sample Exercise "Nutshell" Blank Template